TEACH YOURSELF BOOKS

ARCHERY

Archery is an exciting, fascinating sport, and this book explains right from the start the making of a Master Bowman. Any beginner who really practises the methods explained here should become a skilled archer, or, if already experienced, improve his or her proficiency. Topics covered include the selection and care of equipment; the technique of shooting in a bow; target archery rounds, rules and tournaments; other forms of archery; and making your own equipment.

For those concerned with the administration of archery, this is a valuable reference book. For those who want only to shoot in a bow, it is a handy manual, and it contains enough information about forms of archery other than target archery to whet the appetite. Rounds, rules and tournaments are clearly set out, and include the very important 'unwritten laws' of the sport. All in all, the book will help those who read and digest it to become good archers.

The British Archer

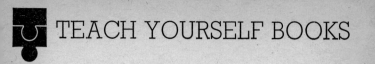
TEACH YOURSELF BOOKS

ARCHERY

Margherita E. Richardson
B.Sc. (Tech.)

ST. PAUL'S HOUSE WARWICK LANE
LONDON EC4P 4AH

First printed 1961
Second edition 1970
Third impression 1971

ISBN 0 340 05510 3

Printed in Great Britain for The English Universities Press Ltd
by Fletcher & Son Ltd, Norwich and bound by
Richard Clay (The Chaucer Press) Ltd, Bungay, Suffolk

Contents

Acknowledgement

THE AUTHOR and publishers wish to thank The Grand National Archery Society for permission to print the RULES OF SHOOTING. The name and address of the secretary is: Mr. J. J. Bray, 20, Broomfield Rd., Chelmsford, Essex.

CHAPTER ONE

Introductory

DRAWING A BOW at a venture ? Yes, that is what you will be doing when you take up the sport of archery, but without the element of risk.

Archery is an exciting, fascinating adventure and once you have fallen under its spell, you will never want to give it up.

You are lucky if you discover its appeal in youth or early middle age, for strength and stamina do play their parts in the making of a Master Bowman, but given modern light equipment it can be said that there is no age limit to the enjoyment to be had from shooting an arrow from a bow.

Archery is a health-giving sport involving no great strain on muscles or heart. It takes you out of doors into the fields and is a complete relaxation from work. Worries are banished from the mind, for to shoot well it is necessary to concentrate all your thoughts on hitting the centre of the target. It seems also to satisfy some primitive instincts in man, instincts which lie buried and may be the cause of vague dissatisfactions with life. You can hit a target and it can't hit back at you !

The beginner is always welcome to shoot on the same target as the experienced archer. He cannot spoil the other's sport, however badly he may shoot, for archery is not a team game. It is an individual test of skill, a private tussle between your will and your reluctant lazy muscles, wandering thoughts and roving eye, for you must discipline yourself to be a good archer, turn your body into a machine and ignore distractions around you.

How long will it take to learn archery? The answer depends on your natural ability, perseverance and the amount of practice you can put in. It is not unknown for an archer to become British Champion in two years. In a summer season you should be able to record an average club handicap and possibly win a club trophy on handicap. But beware of pushing up your scores too quickly at the cost of ruining your future. Be patient, build up a good technique first and know exactly what you are doing consciously. Instinctive shooting is all right for field archery where one shoots at unknown distances but unless you shoot in target archery completely aware of how you are doing it, you will be unable to detect any fault which may creep into your style and then only a good coach can help you.

CHAPTER TWO

History of Archery

No one knows how long ago man first invented the bow and arrow. It was a discovery of major importance to him, for he had learnt how to store energy by using the elasticity of wood. Having tied a string of leather or twisted grass to both ends of a long stick, he bent the stick by pulling on the string so that the energy from his arms became stored up in the thing he had made. By fitting another stick on the string and then letting go, the stored energy was transferred via the string to the smaller stick and away it flew.

When he fastened a sharp, pointed flint to the end of the smaller stick and made it fly further and straighter by fixing birds' feathers to the end of it, he had a weapon much more effective than a stone for killing the wild animals he ate. The prehistoric drawings on the walls of caves of men with bows and arrows are said to be 20,000 years old. Museums are full of flint arrow-heads expertly chipped to thin edges. They are found all over the world, except in Australia where men never realised the possibilities of a bent tree branch. Prehistoric bows have mouldered to dust thousands of years ago but the arrow-heads remain as mute evidence.

Man used his bow and arrows for hunting down his food before he grew some of it by cultivating the soil and rearing cattle, pigs and sheep. He also used the bow to kill his enemies and as man became more civilised he developed it solely as a weapon of war. Read Herodotus, the Greek historian, if you wish to know more about this phase of man's progress. You will find his History, written about 450 B.C., an enthralling, lively source of information about the Archers of Persia, Greece and Asia. He even describes the fortifications of a city built by the Medes. These were built in seven concentric rings, brightly coloured, the first white, the second black, the third red, the fourth blue, and the fifth orange. The two inner rings were plated in silver and gold. The description is so close to our modern target face that one wonders if we owe it to that source.

The invention of gunpowder sounded the knell of the bow as a weapon. Chemical energy took the place of muscular energy to propel the missile and the cannon and musket were devised. But in England and Europe it was several hundred years before the bow was entirely superseded by the gun. The Battle of Agincourt in 1415 was the last great battle won by the strength and skill of the English archers.

Our King Henry VIII regretted the passing of the bow as a weapon and tried to keep archery alive. A keen, highly skilled archer himself, he passed a law that every able-bodied male should practise it. His second wife, Anne Boleyn, used to join him at the shooting butts and in the King's private accounts we find a reference to arrows, shafts, broad heads, bracer and shooting glove for " my Lady Anne ".

Queen Elizabeth I, his daughter, was also a good shot with a bow and is said to have organised a corps of archers among her court ladies. It was her tutor, Roger Ascham, who wrote the first treatise on archery. He published his famous *Toxophilus* in 1545. Written in the English language, it is still worth studying.

Until this royal patronage of archery as a sport, it had belonged to the common man. Although Robin Hood is said by some writers to have been given the title of Earl of Huntingdon when he entered the service of Edward II, it was as the hero of the common people that he won his fame. The singers of the once popular ballads embroidered the stories about him so that it is difficult to untangle fact from fiction, but most legends rest on a basis of fact and there does seem to be sufficient evidence to support the theory that there was a famous outlaw, head of a band of archers, who led a roving life in the forests of Yorkshire and Nottinghamshire early in the fourteenth century. As Robin Hood, he has become the most celebrated archer in English history, and Nottingham City erected a statue to his memory as recently as 1952. Robin's bow, according to the earliest ballads, was buried with him but there still exists in Cannon Hall, Cawthorne, Yorkshire, a bow of spliced yew, 6 ft. 7 ins. long and an estimated pulling weight of 160 pounds. It was obviously used by a very powerfully built man and is reputed to have belonged to Little John, a member of Robin Hood's band. He was 7 ft. in height.

Archery continued to enjoy Royal favour and the Toxophilist Society which was formed in 1780 added Royal to its name when King George IV honoured it with his patronage. Before she came to the throne, Queen Victoria shot with the St. Leonard's Archers and was a member on paper, if not an active one, of the Guild of St. Sebastian at Bruges for fifty years. During her lifetime archery was very popular with young ladies. In August 1845 ladies shot for the first time at a public archery contest. To their consternation, their targets were moved close to the grandstand so that the spectators could see them shoot. Next year there were no lady entrants for the contest ! Archery is no longer only a game for young ladies to be played on the vicarage lawn but has become once again a virile, manly sport.

The Grand National Archery Society was formed in 1861. It lays down the Rules of Archery, holds an annual National Championship and today every club is affiliated to this governing body through the County and Regional Archery Societies. Every club member of an affiliated club is an associate member of the Grand National Archery Society. In England, shooting is mainly confined to target shooting but in America where wild game is still abundant, hunting with the bow is exceedingly popular. The American Archery Society claims that there are one and a half million men and women in that country practising the sport.

Modern archery in England can be said to date from the end of the last world war. The revival of the sport and its increasing popularity has been largely due to the manufacture of the steel bow in this country. Hollow steel tubing was developed and perfected during the war and when peace came, new uses for the product were discovered. With modifications the steel tubing became a bow capable of sending an arrow faster and further through the air with the same muscular effort than the old wooden long bow. Archers who used the new steel bows found their scores increasing and, in 1949, Miss Barbara Waterhouse won the Ladies' World Championships shooting with a steel bow. She made a phenomenal score for those days and with this success put English archery on the sports world map. Today the steel bow has a rival in the modern composite type of bow which is even more efficient at long ranges.

The loom of language has woven many archery terms into the fabric of our daily conversation. We say so and so is " playing fast and loose " when he throws caution aside. Archers cry out " fast " when they mean that to shoot would be dangerous. To loose is to let the arrow fly. A girl making sure of matrimony has " two strings to her bow " and your wife may " let fly " at you if you forget her birthday. If a politician before retiring " shoots his last bolt ", the statement is an echo from the past when bolts were shot from cross-bows. You may be a handy man and put up an extra shelf in the kitchen using " rule of thumb ", an archery term meaning originally the use of the fist with thumb extended to measure the distance between the string and the bow handle.

Perhaps we are rather " wide of the mark " in thinking you might be a handy man but we have given enough examples of the use of archery phrases in everyday conversation to show how prevalent they are. You will probably find yourself using many more.

The bow was revived as a weapon during the last World War. The American Army trained its Commandos in the use of the bow and arrow in jungle warfare. They can kill silently and swiftly at close quarters.

As a sport archery is growing with astonishing rapidity for this Atomic Age. Since 1946 the number of clubs affiliated to the Grand National Archery Society has increased from 10 to 669 and two new bodies to encourage field archery have been formed recently. Known as the British Field Archery Association and The English Field Archery Association respectively, they are open to all members and associate members of the Grand National Archery Society. A National Field Archery Championship is now held every year.

Some archers still shoot in the long bow and the British Long Bow Society exists to perpetuate the use of this historical weapon.

Archery is now included in the Olympic Games.

CHAPTER THREE

Your Equipment

The Bow

THE ARCHERS AT Agincourt shot with their long bows and this type of bow is still preferred by members of the English Long Bow Society. In section it is shaped like the letter **D** and the nocks at each end of the bow are made of horn. Both ends taper. The wood of yew trees was generally used in the past for making long bows and was imported in staves from Italy. English yew grows too slowly and is too full of knots to be of much value. Yew wood when properly seasoned makes excellent long-lasting bows as it is tough and elastic.

The practice bows sold in the shops today are made of fibre glass or lemon wood imported from America. This is a smooth, pale yellow wood having a very fine grain. When the practice bow is pulled, as in the action of shooting, it bends into a simple curve. The bow is flat on both sides, tapers to each end and has an unshaped handle. Some practice bows have an arrow shelf but many have no shelf.

Fibre glass recurved bows of English manufacture are flat on both sides like the wooden bow. The ends are not straight but curve away from the archer when the bow is unstrung. When strung and the bow is pulled, these ends curve in the opposite direction to the rest of the bow and give a much

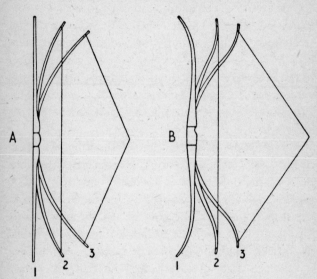

A. Practice Bow.   B. Recurved Bow.
1. Unstrung.   2. Strung.   3. Fully Drawn.

greater propelling force, known as cast, to the arrow than a wooden practice bow. Above the handle is a shelf on which to place the arrow and the bow is fitted with a sighting device.

Experienced archers favour a recurved bow consisting of a laminated wood core, faced and backed with fibre glass or modern synthetic plastic materials, very tough and springy. The principle is not new, laminated recurved bows made of natural materials were in use in Asia hundreds of years ago. These composite bows are being made in England in ever-increasing numbers and have a superior cast to the steel bow, pulling weight for pulling weight. The bow is cut away in the centre so that the position of the arrow on the shelf when shooting is nearer the centre of the bow, thus giving greater accuracy. This type of bow is called a semicentreshot bow. shot bow.

When held in the position of shooting that part of any type of bow facing the archer is called the belly or face of the bow and the opposite is called the back. The part above the handle is known as the upper limb and the part below, the lower limb. The grooves at each end to hold the string are called the nocks. When the bow is strung, the distance between the back of the bow and the string, measured level with the arrow shelf, is referred to as the fistmele, a word you will not find in the dictionary.

The beginner is strongly advised to learn to shoot with a practice bow. It is inexpensive and although it has not the cast of a steel or composite bow, it is quite accurate at short distances. Bows are made in various draw weights, in other words some are easy to pull and others hard to pull. As your muscles will be unaccustomed to pulling a bow,

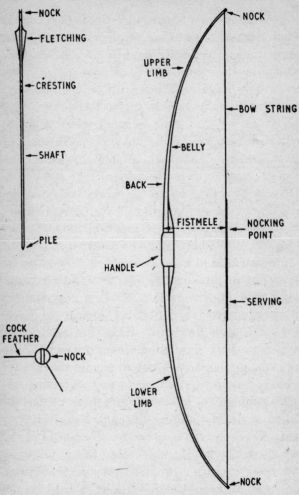

NOCK

FLETCHING

UPPER
LIMB

CRESTING

BELLY

SHAFT

BACK

FISTMELE

HANDLE

PILE

COCK
FEATHER

NOCK

LOWER
LIMB

NOCK

BOW STRING

NOCKING
POINT

SERVING

NOCK

Practice Bow and Arrow.

you will spoil your chances of becoming a good archer right from the start if you try to learn with a heavy bow. You must practise with a light bow to begin with. Would-be archers make mistakes over and over again. They insist on buying or are persuaded into buying, by an assistant who may wish to get rid of unwanted stock, bows of 40 to 50 pounds weight. These are quite useless to the novice archer. The average man needs a bow between 25 and 32 pounds draw weight and a lady 18 to 25 pounds. Later on, when your muscles have developed and you have learnt how to shoot, you should buy a heavier composite recurved bow. This will probably be five times the cost of your practice bow but don't try to economise by buying the more expensive bow to learn with, thus saving the cost of the first one. It is impossible to tell a beginner what weight of bow he will ultimately need. He must find this out for himself first by learning to shoot in the simple wooden or glass fibre bow. THE BOW MUST FIT THE ARCHER. So many inexperienced archers waste their money on buying unsuitable equipment for their strength and length of arm. Bows used for hunting big game must be heavy, for the force required to drive the broad-head arrow deep enough to kill is considerable, but at full draw these bows are only held for a fraction of a second. In target archery the bow sight is held steady on the point of aim for several seconds. Some champions even hold for five seconds or longer. This would be impossible with a 60-pound bow. The average weight of bow used by an experienced archer when shooting at a target is about 36 pounds. The ladies shoot in bows averaging 28 pounds.

Bows vary in length from 5 ft. to 6ft. 10 ins. for adults. The length is not an indication of the weight of the bow, the width also alters the weight. A short bow is a fast bow but too short a bow may be difficult to control and most archers find it better to sacrifice a little speed for the sake of steadiness in the hand when shooting. The shape of bow handles varies also. Some of the modern recurved composite bows on the American pattern have a pistol-grip handle and are fitted with stabilisers.

Arrows

Practice arrows are made of wood and are relatively cheap. A set of six will cost about 30s. The point of the arrow is fitted with a metal pile and the opposite end with a groove or nock which fits on to the string. The arrow is feathered or " fletched " with turkey wing feathers. Two of the feathers or " flights " are of the same colour but the third is usually a different colour. This is the feather which is placed at right angles to the arrow nock. It is called the cock or guide feather. The coloured stripes round the arrow shaft are known as " cresting " and are individual to each archer so that he can pick out his own arrows in the target when shooting with others. Stronger more accurate arrows are made from metal alloy tubing. They are sold in sets of eight, expertly painted and fletched and matched to each other in length, weight and spine. The spine of an arrow is the measure of its flexibility. The heavier the bow, the stiffer the arrow it requires. Bow manufacturers usually specify what length, weight and spine of arrows are recommended for their bows. To shoot a long arrow in a bow made for a short one may break the bow.

The fact that an arrow although shot from the side of the bow apparently flies as if it had been shot through the centre of the bow, has always puzzled archers. This phenomenon, known as The Archer's Paradox, has now been explained by means of slow-motion cinematography. The force of the string hitting the nock of the arrow, bends the arrow. As it tries to straighten out again it takes on an S shape, the fletched end swinging to the left and clearing the bow as it passes. The film clearly demonstrates that the arrow snakes round the bow. After leaving the bow the arrow continues to vibrate and finally settles down to an even flight. If the arrow is too stiff for the bow, it does not bend sufficiently and the arrow fails to clear the bow. If the arrow is too flexible it receives too much initial bend. The spine of an arrow is measured by supporting each end of it and hanging a weight in the centre. The amount of bend is then recorded on a scale. The point of balance of an arrow is usually $1\frac{1}{2}$ to 2 ins. forward of its centre.

The length of arrow you should use depends on the width of your shoulders and the length of your arms. A man with broad shoulders and short arms may need the same length of arrow as a lady with narrow shoulders and long arms. Stretch out your left arm sideways at shoulder level, turn your head, look at your left hand and get someone to measure the distance from your chin to the first joint at the base of your left thumb. This distance gives the length of arrows you require. Arrows vary from 22 to 32 ins. As practice arrows are not sold in half sizes, buy the longer size, not the shorter. For instance, if your chin to thumb base measurement is $26\frac{1}{2}$ ins., buy 27-in. arrows, not 26-in. In fact it is wise to start shooting with arrows apparently too long. As you progress you will probably find your draw length increasing. Too short an arrow can be dangerously overdrawn. You may also bend your left arm too much when using a short arrow thus causing harmful and unnecessary tension which prevents a good follow through and a straight shot. Metal tournament arrows are sold in half-inch sizes, so later on you can buy a set for your composite bow which fit you exactly.

During the last few years archers have been trying

out arrows with four instead of three flights. They give a slightly better sighting point up the bow, that is they actually fly further than three flight arrows of the same weight, length and spine. This is an advantage if your sight is low and only just clears the arrow when shooting at the longer distances. They are also said to be steadier in a wind but having tried them personally, the writer finds no difference between them and three fletched arrows when shooting on a windy day. The traditional feather flights on arrows are being superseded by plastic flights. These never vary like feather flights and resist rain. An arrow rest has to be fixed to the bow about half an inch above the handle when using these plastic flights as they are not flexible enough to pass smoothly over the arrow shelf like a feather flight. In fact without a raised rest they strip off. One well-known firm of arrow makers has compromised by fletching arrows with two plastic and two feather flights, the feather ones only coming into contact with the arrow shelf. Most archers favour the raised rest for use with feather flights also, holding the opinion that it reduces to a minimum any effect of impact on the shelf.

The Quiver

When hunting, archers wear the quiver on the back, but target archers wear it suspended from a belt worn round the waist. The best quivers have separate compartments for each arrow so that the shafts do not touch each other and rattle together. A woollen tassel is worn on the quiver. If your arrow lands in a muddy patch, you then wipe it clean again with your tassel.

Bowstrings

Your practice bow will be provided with a string. This should last for a season but it is wise to have a spare in case it breaks. Until the last few years, bowstrings were made of linen thread and your practice bow may have a linen bow string but very strong synthetic fibres with a breaking strain of 36 lbs. per thread and especially treated to reduce any stretching are now used for bow strings. The string is reinforced or 'served' with coloured thicker linen or nylon thread wound round it for about 8 ins. in the centre. This is to prevent wear at the place where it hits the arm guard. It is also served at the loops. Linen strings are waxed with beeswax to prevent the natural moisture of the linen thread from drying out. Synthetic fibre strings are also waxed to help bind the threads together.

Shooting Glove or Tab

To prevent the bowstring from pressing painfully into the fingers of the right hand and to ensure a smooth loose, a leather shooting glove or tab is worn.

The glove covers the ends of the fingers only and
fastens round the wrist. The palm of the hand is
bare. The tab is made of horse butt and leaves
the backs of the fingers and the hand free. It has
two holes, one slips down to the base of the first
finger, the other to the base of the third finger. It
is then turned back to cover the drawing fingers.
It is a matter of personal preference which type to
buy but the tab is simple, inexpensive and popular.
Choose a smooth, fine-grained one, not too thin.

Arm Guard or Bracer

Shoot without this essential piece of equipment
and you will be painfully aware that the string can
hit your bare left arm stingingly hard and soon
produce a bruise! The jacket sleeve is some
protection but the wide cuff of a jacket will probably
foul your string and spoil your shot. Arm guards
are made of leather, leather cloth or plastic material
fastened with straps or elastic. The best ones are
stiffened down the middle.

Bow Stand

As it spoils any type of bow to lay it down on
damp grass, a stand for your bow is a necessity.
It should take apart so that it may fit into your
tackle case. Do not try to sit on it!

Equipment Case

Many archers make these themselves as they are
fairly expensive to buy. A canvas case will do

instead and the arrows can be carried inside it in the box you bought them in. Ladies may find a canvas archery holdall lighter to carry than the heavier wooden case. Take-apart bows fit into equipment boxes but a long weatherproof bag can be bought in which to carry a bow which is all in one piece.

Clothing

Modern archers have adopted a kind of uniform for club practice days and tournaments. The men wear green or white trousers and green shirts or pullovers. The ladies wear green skirts with white blouses and white woollen jumpers and cardigans. Both sexes wear waterproof and windproof jackets when necessary. White trousers are the correct wear for men at the Grand National Archery Society Championship Meeting. However, for practice shooting most men wear ordinary grey trousers and if you are a lone archer no one is going to worry about what you shall wear. Just see that your clothing does not impede arm movements or catch on the bowstring. You can fold back a too full sleeve and keep it in place with a wide rubber band.

Archery green is best described as a colour midway between Lincoln green and bottle green. It is not a drab olive green and this shade should be avoided.

As there is always the slight danger of a bow breaking when at full draw, it is advisable to wear a cap with a stiff peak when shooting. This is especially important when shooting in a steel bow. The chance of a flat practice bow breaking is remote. Most archers decorate their caps with a collection of badges and other awards.

The Target and Stand

A full-sized target boss and face is 48 ins. in diameter. The boss is made of compressed rye straw. The faces may be of paper, canvas, jute, or paper on a hessian back and they are printed in colours. Faces made of strong bituminised paper are best avoided as they streak the arrows with the black tarry substance. The centre of the target is known to archers as the GOLD—not the bull's eye. It is 9⅗ ins. in diameter and painted yellow or gilded. The rings round the GOLD are red, blue, black and white in that order. Each ring is 4⅘ ins. wide. A GOLD scores 9 points, a red 7, blue 5, black 3, and white 1.

A full-sized target and face costs several pounds, a 24-in. target for practice in a garden correspondingly less, but a beginner on his own can make a serviceable target from a large cardboard box tightly packed with newspaper. It can be suspended from a garage shelf or a tree branch. If you live in the country, you can make a shooting butt with straw

bales and fasten a face to it, but take care to pack
more straw firmly between the bales so that no gaps
are left between them.   You may shoot an arrow
down a gap and lose it.   An old carpet, tarpaulin
or blanket can be used behind a small target or
cardboard box as a back stop.

The target stand resembles an easel.   It is made
of soft wood so that the arrows are not damaged if
they hit it.   When on the stand the centre of the
target should be 4 ft. from the ground and the boss
should slope back at an angle of about 15 degrees.

CHAPTER FOUR

How to Shoot

BEFORE YOU STRING your bow, test your eyesight to determine whether you are going to shoot right or left handed. One archer in ten is left handed.

Do it this way.

Point your finger at your clock, both eyes open, then close your right eye. If your finger appears to move to the right, then you should shoot right handed, holding your bow in the left hand. If, when you shut your left eye, the finger jumps to the left, you will know that the left eye is the one with the dominant sight and you will become a better archer if you shoot left handed. To try to shoot right handed and left eyed is adding to your archery teething troubles.

The left-handed archer holds the bow in his right hand and pulls back the string with his left hand. His arrow is then on the right side of the bow and his right foot is the one nearest to the target. Although this position may seem awkward at first for a naturally right-handed person, most archers soon learn to shoot left handed if they are obliged to do so. A beginner with equally good sight in

both eyes and naturally right handed should shoot
with the bow held in the left hand. If he is
naturally left handed he will probably feel happier
with the bow in the right hand. Shoot with both
eyes open. The right eye of the right-handed archer
will see the point of aim, the vision in the other
eye being automatically suppressed. The archer
shooting left handed suppresses the sight in the right
eye and aims with his left.

Your first practice should be indoors, preferably
in a room with a mirror so that you can check
your positions.

Stringing or Bracing the Bow

See that the lower end of the string is tied firmly
round the nock of the lower limb of your practice
bow, then take a small step forward with the left
foot and place the back of the bottom end of the
bow against the inside of the left foot. Grasp the
handle with the left hand, pull it upwards towards
your body and at the same time press the top of
the right limb down with the palm of the right hand
and slip the top loop of the string into the top nock
of the bow with the fingers. To unstring the bow,
ease the top loop out of the nock in the same way.

A composite bow is strung by a different method.
Fit the lower loop of the string in the lower nock of
the bow and place this nock against the outside
instep of the right foot. The left hand should grasp

the end of the top limb of the bow and the top
loop of the string should be held in the right hand.
Now step over the bow with the left foot so that
the bow presses over the right instep and against
the back of the left thigh.   By pressing the top nock
downwards towards the right hand, the top loop
of the string can be slipped over it.   Alternatively,
you can grasp the top of the bow with the right
hand and bend it across and down so that the
string loop, which is then held in the left hand, can
be slipped over.   This may seem complicated but
it is clear when you try it with the actual bow and
string.   Check the fistmele measurement, twisting
the string clockwise to shorten it and increase the
fistmele and anti-clockwise to unwind the string and
decrease the fistmele.

Shooting Position

In archery you do not face the target.   An
imaginary line joining your heels should pass under
the centre of the gold.   Stand in front of a mirror,
feet about a foot apart, with the bow handle in the
left hand and the left arm hanging loosely by the left
side.   Do not use an arrow yet.   Now bend the left
elbow and bring the bow with the string upper-
most across the body.   With the fingers of the right
hand protected by a shooting glove or tab, place
the first finger above the arrow nocking point on
the string and the second and third fingers below

it. The second finger should be slightly more bent than the third, so that the finger-tips are level. The string should lie across the fingers between the first and second joints.

Turn your head to the left and look your own height, lift the bow to shoulder height, pushing the left arm forward and pulling on the string with the three right-hand fingers at the same time. The left arm should be straight with the elbow turned outwards. The elbow can be locked. Pull the string towards the face until the first finger of the right hand comes under your chin, then press upward firmly on to the chin. The string should touch and press into the chin and lips. This is known as the " anchor " and you *must* get a firm anchor exactly at the same place on your face for each shot. Look in the mirror to see your anchor position, then let your bow down. Do not release the string or you will damage the bow.

Beginners usually find difficulty in pulling the string to the chin because the whole movement involves positions to which the arm muscles are unaccustomed.

As the bow is pulled the pressure of the handle should be felt on the fleshy base of the thumb of the left hand. The thumb itself should lie horizontally and the fingers should lightly encircle the handle. You will find this easier if you drop the wrist and turn the hand up a little but keep that thumb level.

By now you will be eager to dash out of doors to let fly an arrow but curb your impatience and practise this drill for a few days until you are quite sure you can pull the string to your chin and get a firm anchor every time without hesitation. When you do start out of doors, stand 20 yards from your target in the same position, feet apart, shoulders at right angles to your target, bracer on left arm, arrows in the quiver at your right side. Nock an arrow on your bow this way :

Bend the left arm so that the hand and bow handle are against the body at waist height and the string lies over the wrist inside the curve of the arm. Take an arrow in the right hand, the nock pointing to the left, pass the arrow under the bow and fit its nock on to the string at a point directly opposite the top of the handle. This place on the string must be marked with coloured thread. The cock feather should point downwards and the shaft of the arrow lie over the left hand against the bow. If the bow has an arrow shelf, the shaft should be placed on the shelf. Turn the bow over and you are ready to shoot. Not everyone uses this method of nocking an arrow in the bow but when shooting with others you will find it avoids collisions.

Turn your head and look at the gold after you have placed your right fingers on the string, one above and two below the arrow. Draw your bow to the centre of your chin and at the same time let the string roll forward into the first crease of the fingers. This will prevent your arrow from falling away from the bow, a trouble experienced by most beginners. Still keeping your eye on the gold, bring the point of your arrow on to it and hold it

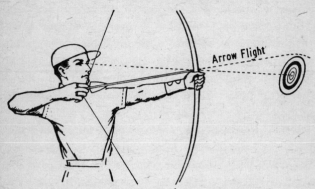

Direct Point of Aim on the Target.
Arrow flies Over the Top.

there steadily for about three seconds. Let your bow down and relax.

Nock another arrow, place the drawing fingers on the string, look at the gold, draw the bow, place the arrow point on the gold, hold it there, then release the arrow by simply opening your fingers. It will probably sail over the target. For the next shot, aim at a point on the ground half-way between you and the target, again holding steadily on this point of aim for three seconds before you release. Do not look at the gold this time but at the point on

the ground.   This time you may hit the target.   If
not, according to where the arrow falls, aim nearer
to yourself or further away.   A piece of white wood
stuck in the ground will give you something definite
to aim at.   In this way you will learn where the
arrow will fall when you aim with its point.   You
can also learn by standing at varying distances from
the target that at one of these distances you can
aim directly at the gold with the arrow point and
hit the target, and that the further away you stand
from this place, the higher you will have to aim to
score a hit.

You will also learn to check your length of draw
with your eye as you must place the pile point on
the mark without taking your eye off the mark and
the two will coincide.   If your arrows fit you correctly the end of the arrow should be in line with
the back of the bow.   After a week or two of aiming
at the mark with the arrow point, you will begin
to draw the arrow to its whole length by feel and
you should cease to check this draw length with
your eye.   Your muscles will do the job for you.
You can now change over to shooting with a sight,
the method used by most experienced archers.   It
is easier and more accurate.

Take a strip of adhesive plaster and stick it
lengthways on the back of your bow just above the
handle.   Push a pin into the strip about 6 ins. above
the handle so that it sticks out $\frac{1}{4}$ in. on the same

side as the arrow. Stand 20 yards away from the
target as before, nock an arrow, look at the gold,
draw your bow, place the pin head on the gold,
hold it there for three seconds very steadily, then
loose.

Do not watch the flight of the arrow, keep your
eye on the gold and your arms up until you hear
the arrow hit the target. Shoot three arrows this
way. If you find they have fallen short of the
target, *lower* your pinsight, if they have gone over
the top, *raise* your pin.

Continue practising at this distance, until your
arrows begin to group. Aim at different places on
the target, not always at the gold. This will give
you more experience of aiming and equalise wear
on the target. Always remember to *hold on your
mark for several seconds* before you loose. It is of
vital importance to start archery with this always
in mind if you wish to become a Master Bowman
and make a real success of your chosen sport. You
will now see why it is essential not to handicap
yourself with too heavy a bow, for holding steadily
on the mark is tiring at first until the muscles have
developed.

Many archers do not hold at all, they snap shoot,
sometimes with surprisingly good results if they have
a keen eye and excellent co-ordination of hand and
eye, but their scores rarely go beyond certain figures
and when they do try to improve by holding on the

aiming point, the poor chaps often find it impossible. They automatically loose as soon as their bowsight touches the gold.

To group your arrows in the centre of the target you must be absolutely still and steady at the moment of release. There must be no wobbling about and no releasing as soon as the sight is on the mark. If there is a secret of success in archery, this is it !

Lower your pinsight $\frac{1}{2}$ in. and shoot at 40 yards. If your arrows group well, move back to 50 yards, and then to 60 yards, adjusting your sight for each distance and practising a week or so at each one. The maximum distance at which your practice bow will shoot using a sight on the target is probably 60 yards. Ladies will find 50 yards the maximum.

CHAPTER FIVE

Target Archery Rounds, Rules and Tournaments

WHEN YOU CAN shoot at 60 yards so that half of your arrows hit the target, it is time to shoot a round.

A good round for beginners is the National Round, 4 dozen arrows at 60 yards, 2 dozen at 50 yards. It can be shot comfortably in $1\frac{1}{2}$ hours. If four people are shooting on one target, each archer in turn shoots 3 arrows, stepping back from the shooting line after he has shot. When all have shot 3 arrows each, the process is repeated until each archer has shot 6 arrows. This is called an " end ". Sometimes, if time is short, two archers shoot together.

The first end is not scored and is known as the " sighter end ". The archers walk up to the target to retrieve their arrows, note where they have hit the target or the ground, return to the shooting line, and make any adjustments necessary to their bow-sights. The next end is scored, each archer writing down his own score in a book if practising only. In a club shoot or tournament, the target captain records the scores on his score sheet.

After 4 dozen arrows at 60 yards have been shot, the archers move forward 10 yards and shoot 2 dozen at 50 yards. No sighters are allowed at this distance during the shoot. A 3rd-class score (men's) for this round is 354, ladies' 3rd-class score, 266, 2nd-class, 321. A man can only be classified as a 2nd-class archer on a round including 80 yards, and as a 1st-Class archer or Master Bowman on a round including 100 yards. A lady archer must shoot rounds including 80 yards to classify 1st-Class or Master Bowman.

You can practise this National Round as a lone archer shooting 3 arrows, retiring 5 paces and then shooting the other 3 arrows, at each end. You can enjoy the sport without the company by trying to beat your own previous score.

The National Round was shot by ladies at the British Championships until 1946. The first lady champion in 1845 won with a score of 186, the last with 625 for a double National Round (2 rounds). The ladies championship is now decided on a double Hereford Round which consists of 12 dozen arrows, the first 6 dozen shot at 80 yards. The other half of the round is the same as the National Round. Men have always shot the York Round in the British Championships.

Here is a list of the most popular rounds shot in the British Isles today :

Round	No. of Arrows (dozen)		Distance (yards)
St. Nicholas	4	at	40
	3	,,	30
	(Boys and Girls under 14)		
Windsor	3	at	60
	3	,,	50
	3	,,	40
	(Juniors under 18)		
American	2½	at	60
	2½	,,	50
	2½	,,	40
National	4	,,	60
	2	,,	50
Western	4	,,	60
	4	,,	50
Albion	3	,,	80
	3	,,	60
	3	,,	50
Long National	4	,,	80
	2	,,	60
Long Western	4	,,	80
	4	,,	60
Hereford	6	,,	80
	4	,,	60
	2	,,	50
St. George's	3	,,	100
	3	,,	80
	3	,,	60
York	6	,,	100
	4	,,	80
	2	,,	60
			(metres)
Fédération Internationale de Tir à l'Arc (F.I.T.A.)—Ladies	3	,,	70
	3	,,	60
	3	,,	50
	3	,,	30
F.I.T.A.—Men	3	,,	90
	3	,,	70
	3	,,	50
	3	,,	30

In the F.I.T.A. Rounds a 4-ft. target divided into
10 rings is used for the 2 longer distances and an
80-cm. 10-ring target for the 2 shorter distances.
No sighters are allowed at any distance. An inner
gold scores 10 and a hit on an inner colour ring
scores one more than when shooting on the ordinary
5-ring target. The F.I.T.A. Rounds are shot in the
World Championships and for the F.I.T.A. Star
onwards.

The Western Round is a favourite with many
archers as both men and women can shoot it
together. It takes approximately 2 hours to shoot.
A Long Western Round, or Men's Western as some
call it, involves shooting at 80 yards and therefore
more time is taken up walking to and from the
target.

The Albion Round gives opportunity to practise
3 distances in an afternoon or evening. This also
applies to the St. George's Round shot by men only.
The Hereford and York Rounds are tests for the
experienced archer. The ladies shoot a double
Hereford Round at the 2-day British Championships
held annually at Oxford, and the men shoot the
double York Round. The longer distances are shot
in the morning and the shorter after lunch.

The Regional Archery Societies—the Grand
Western, the East Midlands, West Midlands,
Northern, Southern, North Wales, South Wales,
Ulster, and Scottish—also hold annual champion-
ships. These usually take place at a week-end and

F.I.T.A., York and Hereford Rounds are shot. Provision is also often made for those archers wishing to shoot a short round only. The combined East and West Midlands Championship is held at Leamington, a town associated with archery contests for over a hundred years. Like the National Championships this is a 2-day shoot and, according to custom, teams representing the East and West Midlands shoot against each other after the championship in the Jephson Gardens, watched by a large crowd of spectators and the Mayor, to uphold archery tradition. The County Societies also have their own championship tournaments every year.

Novices, providing they can shoot at the longer distances, are always welcome at these big shoots and the experience gained is most valuable. However, it is just as well to know several unwritten points of archery etiquette to be observed at any contest, from club to national championship level.

Do not talk to your fellow archers on the same target between ends unless they start the conversation first. Conversation can be distracting to someone who is trying hard to concentrate on each shot and qualify for his Master Bowman's Badge ; just smile and look pleasant. Archers on a target shoot in turn. Be ready when it is your turn to shoot and take your place on the shooting line without delay. If you are shooting with another on the same target at the same time, do not step back immediately you have shot your arrows, wait until your partner has shot his too. Your movement may distract him.

Plant your bow stand at least 6 yards away from the shooting line and if you are obliged to take your dog with you, do tie him up well away from the archers and keep him quiet. If a fellow archer misses the target, do not return to the shooting line until he has picked up all his arrows. If one is missing, help him to look for it. While doing this keep an eye on the rest of the archers and if you see that all are returning to the line, call off the search until a later opportunity. The shoot must not be held up. This is where spare arrows are needed. Always keep a spare string too in your tackle box in case the one you are using breaks and have your box close at hand, not in the pavilion, so that you can put on a new string immediately and not keep your target group waiting.

Never pull out another archer's arrows unless he asks you to do so and never pick them up from the ground. You may think you are being helpful, but a good archer can tell from the position of his arrows on the ground, whether they have gone under or over the target and can adjust his sight accordingly. Pick them up for him and you destroy this useful piece of evidence. If you break another archer's arrow by stepping on it, offer to pay for the damage and if this is accepted, hand over the money on the spot. When an archer succeeds in shooting all of his six arrows into the gold at one end, the lucky person gets an official Six Gold Badge awarded to him by the Grand National Archery Society when the Secretary of this body is informed. The shortest distance for a lady to qualify is 60 yards, for a man 80 yards.

THE GRAND NATIONAL ARCHERY SOCIETY
Rules of Shooting
TARGET ARCHERY

1. *Targets*

   The standard British Target Face is circular, 122 cm. (4 ft.) in diameter. This target is composed as follows: A circle in the centre 24·4 cm. diameter. This circle is ringed by four concentric bands, the breadth of each, measured radially, being 12·2 cm. The colours of the target face are—the central circle Gold, and counting outwards Red, Blue, Black, and White. The centre of the Gold is called the "Pinhole"

2. *Layout*

   (*a*) The targets shall be set up at one end of the ground. They shall be inclined at an angle of about 15 degrees, with the pinholes 4 ft. above the ground.

(*b*) The Shooting Line, over which the archers shall stand, shall be measured from points vertically beneath the pinholes.

3. *Tackle*

(*a*) Any type of hand-bow, other than a cross-bow, may be used. Bows may be changed at will during shooting.

(*b*) Any type of arrow having a smooth pile of a diameter not greater than the shaft at the place of junction may be used. Arrows may be changed at will during the shooting.

(*c*) Arrows must be clearly marked with the archer's name or initials.

4. *Mechanical Releases*

Mechanical releases are not permitted. The Judge may use his discretion in waiving this rule for physically handicapped persons who would otherwise be incapable of shooting.

5. *Aiming*

(*a*) Marks on the bow or on the hand or any form of " pinsight " are permitted ; but bowsights which incorporate any form of lens or prism are not allowed.

(*b*) Artificial points of aim on the ground are permitted, but such must not exceed a height of 15 cm. from the ground or a diameter of 7.5 cm.

(c) Knots or attachments not exceeding a diameter of 1 cm. are permitted on the bowstring.

6. *Shooting*

(a) Shooting shall be from an unsupported standing position except in specially arranged shoots for archers otherwise incapable of shooting.

(b) Six arrows shall be shot at an end. Each archer shall shoot 3 arrows, and when all on a target have shot, shall shoot 3 more.

   If for any reason an archer is alone on a Target, that archer must notify the Field Captain who shall arrange for that Archer to be transferred to another Target or another Archer to be transferred to join the lone Archer.

(c) In the event of an archer shooting by inadvertence more than 6 arrows at an end, the archer shall be penalised by losing the value of his or her best arrow(s) in the target, and such arrows shall not be measured for a Gold prize. If an archer persists in shooting more than 3 arrows consecutively he or she may be disqualified by the Judge.

7. (a) An arrow shall not be deemed to have been shot, if, after leaving the bow, it falls at such a distance from the archer that he or

she can touch the arrow, or portion thereof, with a bow, while one foot is touching the shooting mark.

(b) If from any cause an archer is not prepared to shoot before all have shot, such archer shall lose the benefit of that end.

8. Once an archer has taken his or her position on the shooting line, he or she shall receive no assistance or information by word or otherwise from anyone.

9. *Practice*

(a) At Championship and Open Meetings no practice is allowed on the ground, the same day, except that one end of 6 arrows may be shot as sighters before the beginning of each day's shooting, but only after competitors have come under the Judge's orders at the Assembly. Such sighters shall not be recorded.

(b) No " records " shall be recognised unless shot under Championship conditions.

10. *Control of Shooting*

A Judge or Field Captain non shooting: shall be appointed to take charge of shooting.

11. (a) Unless otherwise directed, No. 3 on each target shall be the Target Captain, and No. 4 the Lieutenant.

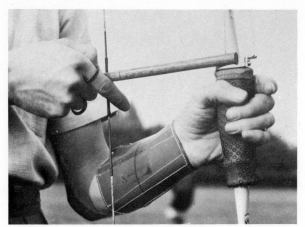

Measuring the fistmele or bracing height of a bow.

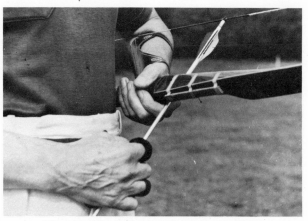

Nocking the arrow on the bow string.

Ready to shoot. Note the position of the fingers.

Position of the bow hand at full draw.

The chin anchor.

Correct method of withdrawing an arrow from the target. The archer on the left is Target Captain and is recording the score.

Archers advancing to the targets to record the scores at the Grand National Archery Championship Meeting. The Field Captain is seen on the left.

Another way to string a composite bow recommended for ladies. The ends of two yards of strong cord are knotted together. Place the cord doubled over the handle and step through both loops. Pull the upper limb of the bow upwards and slip the string loop over the nock. The end of the lower limb is protected from the ground with a car roof rack rubber pad.

Roy Mathews. Master Bowman. British Champion
six times. Member of the British International Team
and Olympic Team.

Miss Lyn Thomas. Master Bowman. British Champion. Holder of the Double Hereford Round Record.
2122.

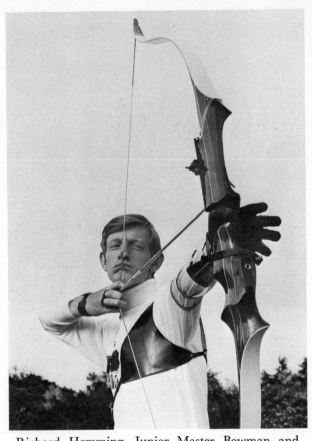

Richard Hemming. Junior Master Bowman and Junior National Champion twice running.

(*b*) The Captain shall be responsible for the orderly conduct of shooting in accordance with the Rules of Shooting, and will enter the scores on the score sheet. The Lieutenant will identify the arrows with the score called and will assist the Captain in any way that may be required.

(*c*) The Target Captain and Lieutenant will check the score sheet and both shall sign it as correct at each distance.

12. (*a*) If any doubt or dispute shall arise it shall be decided by the Target Captain subject to appeal to the Judge.

(*b*) Should the presence of the Judge be required, the Captain or Lieutenant will remain at the target to give any assistance which the Judge may require.

13. *Scoring*

(*a*) The scoring points for hits on the target are : Gold 9, Red 7, Blue 5, Black 3, White 1. The same shall be determined by the position of the arrow shaft.

(*b*) If an arrow touches two colours it shall be scored as in that of the higher value.

Neither the arrow nor the target face shall be touched until the final decision has been given, and any interference with the target or arrow shall disqualify the archer from scoring the higher value.

14. (*a*) An arrow passing through the target or rebounding from it cannot be scored.

   (*b*) An arrow passing through the target face but remaining in the boss shall be withdrawn by the Captain or Lieutenant and shall be inserted from the back in the same place and at the assumed angle of original penetration until the pile is visible in the target face, when the score shall be determined.

   (*c*) An arrow hitting and remaining embedded in another arrow shall be scored the same as the arrow struck.

   (*d*) An arrow on the ground believed to have hit and rebounded from another arrow shall be scored the value of the struck arrow, if the latter is found in the target with its nock damaged in a compatible manner.

   (*e*) An arrow in the target, which has or may have been deflected by another arrow, shall be scored according to the position of its shaft in the target face.

15. No alteration shall be made in the value of an arrow as entered on the score sheet, to the advantage of its owner after such arrow has

been drawn from the target. No arrows shall be drawn from the target until all the archers' scores shall have been entered on the score sheet, and the Captain is satisfied that they are correctly entered, without the express direction of the Captain.

16. An archer may delegate another archer on the target to record his score and to pick up his arrows.

17. In club shoots, scores for handicap and classification purposes or for six-gold badges may only be returned when a minimum of two archers are shooting together in order that the score sheet may be witnessed and signed.

   Distances must be shot in their correct sequence and on the same day.

18. *International Rounds*

   When shooting F.I.T.A. Rounds, F.I.T.A. Rules shall apply.

19. *Safety*

   A loaded bow may not be drawn except on the shooting line and in the direction of the target.

20. Archers, other than those actually shooting or moving to or from the shooting line, shall take

up their positions at least 5 yards behind the shooting line.

21. The Judge or Field Captain shall indicate when each end is completed and no archer shall advance from the line before receiving the signal.

The Handicap System

The system of classifying archers into proficiency groups—Master Bowman, first, second and third class—is, with the exception of the Master Bowman class, being replaced by a system of handicapping based on an archer's scores. Copies of the Handicap Tables may be obtained from the Secretary of the Grand National Archery Society, price $12\frac{1}{2}$p (2/6)*.

An archer should know his handicap number as soon as he has shot five rounds on Club Target Days or outside Tournaments and Championships according to all the G.N.A.S. Shooting Rules. These rounds need not be all the same.

The Regional and County Archery Societies, as well as the G.N.A.S., are now asking for the entrant's handicap number on entry forms for Championship Shoots, as medals and trophies are often also awarded on handicap. Many clubs are also basing awards on scores plus handicap allowance and the Club Captain keeps a Record Book of scores and each

* See Acknowledgement, page vi.

member's handicap number, re-assessing it every few weeks or so to keep it up to date.

Only scores of rounds shot strictly to G.N.A.S. Rules are of use for estimating handicap. A practice score recorded by the archer himself does not count and it is to the advantage of every archer to remember this and to keep to the rules. Compare your own scores shot when practising with those shot at organised Club Shoots and outside tournaments and you will probably see that your practice scores are higher. Shooting in competition with others imposes a nervous strain. Some lucky archers are not affected but the majority of us do suffer to some extent.

CHAPTER SIX

Improving Your Scores

Now you know the basic method of shooting in a bow, the archery terms and rules and you can proceed to learn the finer points of technique.

When practising you may have realised that an archer shoots with his legs as well as his arms. Your weight should be divided equally between both legs and you should place it on your heels rather than on your toes. If you find you are standing on uneven ground, move your position until you feel comfortable. One foot up hill and the other down hill will throw your body out of balance and make shooting more difficult. Look at the position of your feet at every shot and correct it if necessary, always keeping your feet on a line which is at right angles to the target and parallel to each other. One foot can creep in front of the other during an end.

As the arrow must be placed on the string in exactly the same place at every shot, the nocking point on *all* your strings should be clearly marked. The usual way is to wind coloured thread round the string at the bottom of the point. It is not necessary to put thread above as well. If your arrows tend to fall off the string before you draw the bow, wind dental floss over the nocking point. Remember to mark your point $\frac{1}{8}$ in. above the arrow rest on the bow to give clearance to the arrow flights and do see that the fistmele height is correct for your type of bow. A large set square is useful for marking the nocking point. Do not rely on your eye alone.

If your bow has no arrow shelf, glue a small piece of wood, about $\frac{1}{4}$ in. wide and the width of the bow immediately above the handle on the left side. Alternatively you can glue on a feather shelf or rest made with a piece of a flight reinforced with another narrower flight underneath it. An arrow shelf is not absolutely necessary as the arrow can be supported over the left hand, but it does ensure that the arrow is placed in exactly the same position in the bow every time and gives greater accuracy.

After you have drawn your bow and are standing for those few seconds quite steady, aiming and holding, there is a delicate balance between your left and right arms. You are pushing with your left and pulling with your right, equal and opposite forces are in a state of equilibrium. Push too much with the left arm and you will get an involuntary release as the string is pulled off the right fingers, pull too much with the right fingers and your left arm will come across your body as you release, making your shot fly to the right. Try to feel this balance, be aware of it with every arrow right up to the moment of loosing. It is actually part of the loose.

Ideally your right forearm, wrist and back of the hand should be *in line with the arrow* horizontally. To achieve this, however, may be difficult for some archers for it largely depends on the relative lengths of forearm and upper arm. The upper right arm is bound to come out of line because you are anchoring on the chin, so don't worry about it. Pull the right elbow back with the shoulder muscles after the draw until you feel *inside* the bow. It is a grand feeling especially if you see your arrow land in the gold after the loose because you have managed to get in line. Remember to keep your body upright as you shoot. You should not lean forwards or backwards from the waist, in fact your trunk should not move at all, all the pulling and pushing should be done with the arms and shoulders. Beginners often strain backwards when shooting at the longer distances, so guard against this becoming a habit.

In-line shooting is most important for consistently high scores. Check your position in front of the mirror occasionally or get your wife or a friend to look down on you from an upstairs window or over the stair banisters as you draw an arrow. Some coaches advise the archer to draw the shoulder-blades together while holding on the mark.

The position of the bow arm may give you some trouble at first. The shoulder should be kept low not hunched up. At the moment of release the bow arm should not be kept rigid and prevented from moving to the left and downwards. This is the natural reaction if the archer is using his back and shoulder muscles fully. These muscles must be strong and tireless. If the arm moves to the right across the body, the back muscles are relaxing just before the release because they are tiring. Keep your arms up after the release, holding the follow through and look at their position at every shot.

You may hear a lot of advice about relaxing this or that part of the body as you shoot. The verb " to relax ", according to the *Oxford Dictionary*, means to cause or allow to become loose or slack or limp. The advice is confusing. It is tension, that is unnecessary muscular effort, which you should avoid. Relax your muscles between shots, let your arms swing loosely, drop your head and close your eyes if you like. Many archers do this as it helps to overcome tension. Relax the muscles of your face too, there is no need to frown or push your lips forward to meet the string. Above all relax your mind.

If you have arrows which are the right length for you, you should draw them back so that the end of the arrow pile is level with the back of the bow. If, when you are comfortably drawn, your arrow, being too long for you, sticks out $\frac{1}{4}$ in. or so in front of the bow, do not worry. Underdrawing in this way will not affect your shooting but you must draw the same length each time and hold steady. If you "creep ", that is allow the arrow pile to go forward towards the target as you hold, the shot will be a low one; conversely, if you overdraw, the shot will go high. Creeping can be avoided by pulling the string firmly into the chin using the shoulder muscles and remembering to pull with the third finger as well as with the other two. Guard against over-drawing ; apart from causing high shots, it can cause accidents.

A strip of cork or adhesive plaster fastened to your bow and a pin makes a sight for a beginner but more accurate sights are fitted to tournament bows. The sights have a metal geared pin sliding up and down a groove in a plastic or metal strip. Expensive? Yes, but easier to operate as fine adjustment can be made in and out as well as up or down.

The simplest way to loose an arrow is to straighten the fingers of the drawing hand. The hand and fore-arm will then move backward, *still in line*. If you are pulling really hard with your back and shoulder muscles as well as pushing with your bow arm, your hand should fly right back behind your head. If the right hand moves out of line away from your face, your shot may be a bad one and may miss the target altogether. Try not to drop your hand either, and keep the fingers together as you straighten them, not spread wide apart. Beginners sometimes twist the string at the loose. This should not happen if you think of the fingers as hooks and the back of the hand, wrist, and forearm as a rigid bar without joints. Do not cup the jaw between the thumb and forefinger as this interferes with a clean loose. The end of the first finger should be under the chin and the thumb held low.

Perhaps you may be thinking at this point, "Heavens, what a lot to remember. I can't think of all that at every shot!"

But you will, you know.

Not at first, but it all comes with practice. Some of the things you will do each time almost without conscious thought, but you are thinking about them just the same.

Well, let's proceed, you can learn a lot more.

At full draw, you will not see the string because you should be concentrating your gaze on the aiming mark, but you should know its position relative to the front of the bow so that you can check and correct it, if your scores fall. With many archers the string lines up with the left side of the bow or a little to the right of it. It is not advisable to shoot with a gap between the bow and the string, "a window" as archers call it. If there is a gap, you cannot check the exact position of your string and may shoot badly to the right. Find the correct string position to put your arrows in the centre of the target and stick to it. Do not try to adjust your aim by altering your string position, alter your sight instead.

Go to an archery tournament and you will see many different positions of the left hand holding the bow. You have already been given the grip which is recommended for beginners. Make slight variations to it if you feel more comfortable that way. A slight shifting of the hand round the bow to the left may prevent the string hitting your left arm and give a cleaner shot. But whatever you do, see that the thumb remains horizontal. This is a little point, but that thumb prevents the bow twisting to the right as you release.

Try to keep your grip loose. A hard tense grip absorbs the energy of your bow and your shot will be lifeless and low on the target. Let the stored energy in your bow at full draw release itself freely. You will soon notice the difference. It is possible to shoot without gripping the bow at all so that it falls to the ground after every shot. Try it as an experiment and adopt the idea if it causes your scores to increase, using a bow sling round your wrist to prevent the bow from falling. Many Master Bowmen shoot with an open hand, the handle of the bow pressing only on the ball of the thumb. You may find it helpful to put a little top pressure on the handle in order to get a nice straight shot.

You will see archers draw their bows with the

arrow pointing to the skies, then bring their pinsight down on to the gold. Others draw to the left and bring the sight across on to the gold. All this is wasted energy. From waist level, bring your bow-sight up on to the gold, slowly and deliberately, keeping your eye on the gold all the time and drawing your string back to your chin without any movement of your head. Remember your first finger should be under your chin, and touching it, the string pressed into the chin.

Your sight is now on the gold. Feel for the balance between the arms, pull your shoulders back so that you are in line and inside the bow, press towards the target, hold steady on the gold and release. *Do not follow the flight of the arrow.* Continue to look at the gold until you hear a satisfactory " plop " of the arrow hitting the target and keep your arms up. Following the flight of the arrow to see where it is going upsets the eye and mark relationship and the feeling that the archer is " willing " the arrow into the gold. It may engender the bad habit of raising the head as the arrow is loosed, thus causing a high shot.

Archery can be so fascinating that beginners often practise every day whatever the weather. One must get used to shooting in wind of course but do your practice on calm days whenever possible. Your score is then a direct indication of your form and groups to the left or right of the centre not due to wind deflection but faults in your technique. The wind gets blamed too often for bad shooting.

However, when you are shooting in a competition, wind is often an unavoidable handicap. A gale can play havoc with scores, especially if in addition to blowing the arrow, it blows the archer's arm off his aim just as he is releasing the arrow. Try standing with your legs further apart and your knees and toes turned inwards on a very windy day. Your stance will be much firmer. Experienced archers say, " find your point of aim on a windy day and stick to it ". Don't try to allow for wind variations. Wind gusts may be at your end of the field and not at the target end. If you have some, use heavier arrows. A strong head wind can lower your sight as much as $\frac{1}{2}$ in. ; conversely, a following wind can raise it.

If it rains as well as blows, you can treat your arrow flights with a preparation used by fishermen to keep their fishing flies dry or use a set of arrows with plastic flights and a raised feather arrow rest on your bow.

Finger tabs and gloves give a poor release when soaked with rain. Keep yours in your pocket between ends and change to a dry tab as often as you can.

Do not be in too great a hurry to shoot at the longer distances when you get your new composite bow. It takes time to get used to a new handle and the " feel " of a new bow. As a member of a club it's tempting to enter for the various handicap shoots and competitions in the season's programme, but for some weeks keep to the National Round. Do a bit of quiet practice too on your own at 30 yards, until you can hit the gold six times out of six. It looks a lot bigger at this distance ! In this way you will learn to control your new bow and also that part of your mind which should be concentrating carefully on each shot. This private practice is worth many evenings shooting with a happy-go-lucky crowd. You can join them later when you can slam your arrows home easily at 60 yards.

Always, even when practising, shoot according to the G.N.A.S. Rules. They have been devised with an end in view, to make archery a safe, enjoyable, dignified sport, not a casual playing about with a bow and arrow. That pause after the first three arrows have been shot, while the other chap has his turn, is sensible. It gives your mind and muscles a rest and you will shoot better for it. To shoot six arrows all at once, as some archers unfortunately do, leads to hurried shooting and bad reflex habits against which the conscious will can be powerless, an annoying and frustrating state of affairs. When on your own, turn and walk five paces away from the shooting line between your two groups of three arrows.

Men strive to improve performance in all sports and games and archery is no exception. Apart from the vastly more efficient bows which have been designed in the last few years, various gadgets have been invented. The 'clicker' is one of these. It consists of a narrow strip of metal fastened to the left side of the upper limb of the bow. The arrow is inserted between it and the bow and the archer draws the arrow until the pile slips past the metal strip with an audible click. This triggers off the release.

The advantage to the archer of the clicker is that he cannot allow his arrow to creep forward. He must continue to push and pull until he hears the click before he can release. All this time he is holding steadily on the mark and at the moment of release his arrow is not moving forward, an ideal state of affairs. The beginner should try to do without a clicker until he has established a good form and possibly never need one if his scores continue to improve but if he comes to a point where nothing seems to help his progress, then he should try a clicker. The initial difficulty is finding the place on the bow to fix it. Put it too far back towards your face and you will pull in vain to make it click, possibly shoot through it in desperation and damage your flights. Stick it too far forwards and you may draw right through it. Only by experimenting will you find the exact spot. Providing that you shoot correctly otherwise, your scores must improve when shooting with a clicker. Archers of World Championship standard owe their magnificent scores to this small invention so that it is worth while perservering until you have mastered its use.

To help to get the bow string centred on the face, some archers use a kisser. This is a small bead on the string, diameter not more than 1 cm. according to G.N.A.S. Rules. The kisser is anchored on the mouth.

Now the trouble with kissers is that they can slip up or down the string and thus upset your aim. Make a kisser by cutting a strip of adhesive plaster $\frac{1}{4}$ inch wide, separate the strands of the string at the point where you want your kisser, slip one end through the string, press firmly, then wind the rest of the strip round the string to make the bead. This way it cannot slip.

Watch an archer shooting with a kisser and you will probably see that he unconsciously reaches for it with his lips so that he fails to draw the string firmly into his chin. This is the danger, so be on your guard and try to do without it.

Archers who take their sport really seriously shoot with binoculars hanging round their necks. With these they check the position of every arrow they shoot. The author does not suggest that everyone must adopt this idea but binoculars *are* useful to check the sighting arrows. If the first arrow is seen to be low on the target, the sight can be lowered and if this adjustment is not sufficient for the second arrow, lowered still further and so on. It is most annoying when shooting at the longer distances to find one's sighter arrows have all grouped much too high or too low, and after moving the sight, the first half-dozen arrows are still not in the centre. The first arrows shot after the change down to the shorter distances should also be checked with binoculars if they cannot be seen in the target with the naked eye. Most archers have marks on their bows to indicate the approximate positions of sights at various distances but you will always find some adjustments are necessary. Distances are very often paced out instead of accurately measured and the 60 yards distance, for instance, may actually be anything from 60 to 65 yards.

Record your scores when practising in a proper score book ruled for the purpose. As the weeks pass you will see how you have progressed and the mental arithmetic involved in adding up your dozens is good practice for the day when it's your turn to be Target Captain. Keep a note too of any special points you notice which improve your shooting so that you can refer back to them. You may easily forget unless you write them down.

Shoot at balloons fastened to the target for a change and a bit of fun as well as practice in careful, accurate aiming. You *must* hold steady to burst a balloon. Above all always remember that archery is a sport to be enjoyed. If your scores go down, don't take it too seriously ; have a complete rest from archery for a week, then go back to first principles and start again, checking every point. Even Master Bowmen go through bad patches of form. A coach can be a help to spot an obvious fault but even he cannot see your string position as you see it or get inside your mind to understand any mental difficulty. There is no easy road to success in archery. However, most old hands in a club will lend a sympathetic ear to a beginner's troubles, so do not hesitate to ask their advice. You will find they seldom offer it unless asked.

CHAPTER SEVEN

Care of Equipment

THIS INFORMATION MIGHT have been included in the chapter on improving your scores. No one can expect to shoot well with a misshapen bow and bent arrows with missing flights.

Look after your bow most carefully. If it takes apart, you can keep it in your tackle box, otherwise buy a waterproof case for it. Store it when not in use in an unheated room. Never lend your bow to a novice. Before you realise what he is doing he may draw it and loose without an arrow, thus shortening its life. Experienced archers never expect a fellow archer to lend his bow. Lending a discarded practice bow is another matter. Buy a waterproof case for your bow and a couple of rubber bow tip protectors. Store it when not in use in an unheated room. Central heating is particularly bad for wooden bows. It can make them so brittle, they may break easily when fully drawn. With care a bow should last for about four years or possibly longer, depending on the amount of shooting you have done with it. After that time it may lose cast. If you are ever doubtful about the condition of your bow after several years' use, it can be returned to the makers for examination and advice.

Composite bows are guaranteed for one year. A good one should last as long as a fibre glass bow if never overdrawn or otherwise misused. String it gently and smoothly according to the maker's instructions while standing on soft grass or a mat. If the end of the bow comes in contact with hard concrete it may be damaged. Never leave a composite bow exposed to hot sunshine and cover it when it rains. Wipe it dry before putting it away in its canvas case and give it a rub over occasionally with furniture cream.

Remember to check the bracing height of the string on your bow whether it is a fibre glass or a composite. It harms a bow to shoot with it underbraced or overbraced.

Your wooden bow is practically indestructible given normal use. It may follow the string, that is develop a permanent curve at either end and lose cast but it will still be usable. Do not sell it when you pass on to a better bow. Lend it to beginners. Go back to it and start again if your archery breaks down and you cannot find the reason for it. You may also find it useful for practising at short distances when the weather is too bad for outside shooting.

Arrows

Even the best and toughest arrows bend if they hit a nail in the target stand, or a stone on the ground or the target blows off the stand with your arrows in it. (Yes, that *can* happen at shoots, so take a look at the target fastenings on a windy day.)

Bent arrows can be straightened in an apparatus known as an arrow straightness tester and straightening aid. The actual straightening of the shaft is carried out by fingers and thumb pressure while the arrow is in the straightener and the degree of straightness is noted on a gauge. Although efficient the cost of the apparatus is rather high for the individual archer. It is possible to get your arrows straightened and reconditioned by the manufacturers of one leading make of arrows. They are returned looking like new ones. Have this done in the autumn months when they are not so busy. It costs less then.

If your arrows get streaked with a black tarry substance from the target face, clean it off with turpentine substitute or paraffin. Do not use steel wool as this may remove the plating or protective lacquer on the arrows.

Keep a tube of colourless adhesive in your tackle box and replace flights as soon as they become unstuck. This adhesive is also useful for replacing loose nocks.

Pull an arrow out of the target by placing the first and second fingers of the left hand on either side of it, then press on the target with these fingers and pull out the arrow with the right hand. This avoids bending it. Serious damage can be caused to arrows by roughly dragging them out of the target. If an arrow has almost passed through the boss, pull it right through from the back of the target. The flights will emerge unharmed. When an arrow penetrates the wood of the stand, lever it out by gripping it close to the pile, then moving the arrow up and down several times before pulling it.

Lost Arrows

Arrows can " snake " in the grass, burying themselves almost completely out of sight. A heavy metal rod is useful for locating missing arrows. Scrape the grass with it firmly, working backwards and forwards both in front of the target and behind. If systematic close search fails to find the missing arrow, shoot another to miss the target as you think the other one may have done and get someone to watch intently where it strikes the ground. Search in this spot and you will probably find the first one. Shakespeare knew this dodge. You will find it described in *The Merchant of Venice*.

Remember that after a dry spell of weather or when the ground is hard with frost, arrows can slither along the grass a long way behind the target.

Avoid shooting at a moving object on the ground, a balloon bobbing across the grass for instance. If you miss, and you probably will, you may have great difficulty in finding the spot where your arrow lies. Mark every arrow with your name. You can buy transfers for this purpose.

Wipe your arrows clean with your tassel if they get muddy and rub the shafts with an oily rag when you get home. The oil helps them to slip easily out of the target face.

Bowstrings

A linen bowstring which has become too dry is much more liable to break than one which has retained its natural moisture in the threads. Keep your strings in an air-tight tin to prevent them drying out. Use them in turn and at the first signs of a fraying thread, wax the string, but do not do this too vigorously or you will generate frictional heat and dry out the very moisture you wish to keep in ! Replace serving when it unravels for the string will quickly wear at the point where it hits the arm guard if it is unprotected by serving thread.

A Dacron string should last a year. Discard it if a thread breaks for this may be a sign that it is wearing under the serving at the nocking point, a place where strings often break when worn out. If the arrow lands in the target after the string breaks, no harm will come to the bow as the force has been transferred to the arrow but a string breaking at the loose *can* sometimes damage a bow, so do not take risks and shoot with a worn-out string.

Do all the little repair jobs before you put away your equipment after a shoot. You may forget all about them until you open your tackle box on the archery field again. You have been warned !

CHAPTER EIGHT

Other Forms of Archery

Clout Shooting

THIS IS LONG-DISTANCE shooting at a large target marked out on the ground. Originally the clout was a piece of cloth or canvas stretched on a wooden frame. Clout shooting is a pleasant variation from ordinary target shooting. To avoid the trouble of marking out the rings on the ground the following procedure can be adopted. When all the competitors have shot, the Field Captain fastens the end of a rope to the flag in the centre of the clout area. The rope is coloured gold, red, blue, black and white in sections in the correct lengths and as it is moved taut round the flag, it touches the arrows and the appropriate score for each one can be recorded.

When shooting at the clout the bow is elevated to about 45 degrees. A simple sight made from a piece of sticking plaster can be fixed to the lower limb of the bow about 8 ins. below the handle. This can be lined up with the flag or with any suitable point of aim behind the clout. A change of about 15 ft. in the height of the point of aim above the flag will cause your arrow to land 6 ft. further from the previous point of impact of the arrows when shooting at 180 yards. Raise your bow by bending back from the waist. The arms stay in the same position relative to the shoulders as in target archery.

G.N.A.S. Clout Shooting Rules

The Target Shooting Rules shall apply with the following special provisions :

1. The target shall be measured on the ground in the proportion of six times the size of a standard target. Scoring 5, 4, 3, 2, 1, for each colour.
2. The centre of the target shall be marked with a light coloured flag not more than 6 inches from the ground.
3. The standard distances are,
   For men, 8 to 10 score yards.
   For ladies, 6 to 8 score yards.
   but other distances may be shot. A round consists of 36 arrows.
4. Six arrows shall be shot at an end.
5. Shooting may be either "two way" or "one way".
6. Only the appointed scorers are permitted to enter the area of the target until they have scored and drawn all arrows.

Flight Shooting

An arrow may be shot much further with a specially designed flight bow than with a target bow. A sipur is used with a flight bow. This is an extension of the arrow shelf and it enables the arrow to be drawn back into the bow so that the maximum bow cast is obtained. Considerable skill is required to get the best out of a flight bow as well as muscular strength. The National Flight Championships are held every year after the National Target Archery Championships. The present record for flight bows is 606 yards men, 371 yards ladies.

Target bows are also used for flight shooting in competition but as it is fairly obvious that a bow of 40 pounds will shoot an arrow further than a bow of 30 pounds, competitors should be divided into classes according to their bow weights.

G.N.A.S. Flight Shooting Rules

1. The three classes for which competitions may take place are :
   A. Target Bows.
   B. Flight Bows.
   C. Free-style.

The classes may be sub-divided into bow weights if desired, the bow weight being the actual or calculated weight at full draw. For classes A and B, only hand bows may be used and the bow must be held in the unsupported hand.

If competitions for both target and flight bows are being held on the same occasion, all shooting with target bows must be completed first.

2. (a) A target bow is any bow with which the user has shot at least two target rounds. In the event of a breakage, a similar bow may be used as a replacement.

   (b) Any type of bow, other than a cross-bow, may be entered for Classes B and C.

3. (a) In the target-bow class competitors must use their own length standard target arrows.

   (b) In Classes B and C any type of arrow may be used.

4. Sipurs are not permitted in Class A.

5. Mechanical releases are not permitted.

6. Competitors should be at least 6 ft. apart, and must not advance their leading foot over the shooting line.

7. Each competitor must have one assistant or adviser, who must keep at least 1 yard behind the shooting line.

8. There shall be a Range Captain in charge who will act as referee and judge. His decision shall be final. He will also be responsible for the safety of onlookers, who must at all times, when shooting is in progress, be not less than 10 yards behind the shooting line.

9. The range line, which is at right angles to the shooting line, must be clearly marked at 150

yards, and then at 50-yard intervals to the maximum distance required. In the far distance, a suitable aiming mark such as a target or a large white board should be provided.

10. Measurement of distances shall be made along the range line with a steel tape. The distance shot shall be measured to that point on the range line at which a line at right angles to the range line passes the point where the arrow enters the ground. If the arrow is lying on the ground, the line should pass through the pile end of the arrow.

11. National records may only be claimed in respect of Classes B and C, and the measurements must be checked and witnessed by the Range Captain and one other responsible person. In addition the Range Captain must certify that the ground over which the shot was made is reasonably flat and level. No record will be recognised unless it beats the existing record by a yard or more.

Field Archery

Given a pleasant area of open country, a fine sunny day and good company, field archery can be a very satisfactory substitute for hunting with the bow and arrow. The targets or life sized animal targets are placed round the course at definite distances but as these can be unknown to the archers taking part, aiming is not easy. This type of archery appeals to the archer who has a good eye for judging distances correctly and can aim instinctively. The chin anchor can be abandoned and the arrow drawn just below the eye. The archer may also guess the distance and shoot with a sight as in target shooting. As you will probably have a good many misses at the targets, take old arrows with you when you go on a field shoot and cheerfully abandon a fruitless search for lost arrows. If you are the organiser of a field shoot, omit the longer distances for beginners in this variation of archery. In real hunting the archer gets as close to his quarry as he can before loosing the arrow.

Instinctive or bare bow shooting can be acquired by practice but as field shooting is only just gaining in popularity in England, the archer may have to travel long distances to enter field archery competitions. Many clubs, however, hold a field archery shoot every year as a change from shooting the usual target archery rounds. A few clubs have given up target archery in favour of field.

G.N.A.S. Field Archery Rules

Targets

1. Four face sizes shall be used.
   (*a*) A 24-in. face with a 12-in. centre ring and a 4-in. aiming spot.

(b) An 18-in. face with a 9-in. ring and a 3-in. spot.

(c) A 12-in. face with a 6-in. ring and a 2-in. spot.

(d) A 6-in. face with a 3-in. ring and a 1-in. spot.

The outside ring shall be black. The centre ring shall be white and the aiming spot shall be black.

Alternately animal targets bearing these round faces may be used, in which case the faces need not be painted, only outlined. The aiming spot must be plainly visible. The spot must be painted white or some colour sharply contrasting with the target colour.

Layout

2. A standard course shall consist of the following 56 shots (4 arrows from each of 14 stands) :

(a) 15, 20, 25 and 30 yards at 12-in. face.

(4 arrows at each distance.)

40, 45 and 50 yards at 18-in. face.

(4 arrows at each distance.)

55, 60 and 65 yards at 24-in. face.

(4 arrows at each distance.)

4 arrows at 35 yards at an 18-in. target; all at the same distance, but from different positions or at 4 different targets.

1 arrow each at 30, 35, 40 and 45 yards at an 18-in. face.

1 arrow each at 50, 60, 70 and 80 yards at a 24-in. face.

1 arrow each at 20, 25, 30 and 35 ft. at a 6-in. face.

(b) In laying out the Course, the 14 stands, and the various Positions at four-positions stands, may be arranged in any order at the discretion of the organiser.

(c) A 5% variation in distance is permitted where necessary because of terrain. All shortages, however, must be made up at another stand or position on the course.

(d) All butts must be so placed that the full face is exposed to the archer.

(e) Posts at each stand shall be numbered, but the distances must not be given.

Tackle

3. Any kind of bow, except a cross-bow, and any kind of arrow, except broadheads or arrows that would unreasonably injure a target face, may be used in any event unless otherwise stated.

Aiming

4. In any tournament in which free style and instinctive archers have separate classes :

Archers shooting in the instinctive class must use bows free from any sights, marks or blemishes that could be used in aiming. This applies to the string also.

In the free-style class any type of sight may be used except one calibrated for the course.

5. In tournaments where no distinction is made between the two styles of shooting, the only sight that shall be allowed is a single narrow mark, not exceeding ⅛ in. in width or a single fixed sight of similar dimensions.

6. At no time and in no class shall any device be allowed that would in any manner be of aid in estimating the distance of any shot. Nor may the archer refer to any memoranda of any kind that could in any manner be a means of improving his or her score.

Shooting

7. Archers shall shoot in groups of 4, if possible, otherwise in groups of not less than 3 or more than 5.

8. Each archer shall shoot 4 arrows at each of the 14 stands on the Course. In 10 cases this shall mean shooting 4 arrows from a single post at a single face. In the other 4 it may mean either shooting 1 arrow from each of 4 posts at a single face, or 1 arrow at each of 4 separate faces from a single post.

9. No one shall approach the target until all of the group have finished shooting.

10. Shooting shall be in the order of the scores made at the previous stand, i.e. highest scorer first, etc. In case of a tie the Target Captain may state the order of shooting. When the course allows, two may shoot at a time and it is highly recommended that all courses be laid out to allow for this.

11. One group shall not hold up the following groups while looking for lost arrows. Enough arrows shall be carried so that each archer may continue shooting and return later to find missing arrows. Alternatively, the following group may be called through.

12. An archer who has to stop shooting because of a broken string or similar cause must take witnesses, appointed by the Field Captain, with him when he completes the round.

13. Where applicable G.N.A.S. Rules concerning safety shall be observed.

Control of Shooting

14. A Field Captain shall be appointed and he shall :
    (*a*) See that a Target Captain and one Scorer is appointed for each group.
    (*b*) Designate the order in which groups are to shoot or assign the stand from which each group is to start, depending on which system is used.

(c) Be the final authority in settling any disputes that may arise over rules or conduct of the tournament.

15. The duty of the Target Captain shall be (a) to certify the score card, and (b) to settle all local questions. His decision on arrow values shall be final. Other decisions may be referred to the Field Captain.

16. A scorer shall keep account of every arrow that hits the target on the official score card obtained from the Secretary.

Scoring

17. The scoring shall be 5 points for the centre ring including spot, and 3 for the outer ring.

18. The status of doubtful arrows shall be determined before drawing any arrows from the target, and such arrows may not be touched until after being recorded.

19. The Target Captain shall be the final judge of all disputed arrows.

20. An arrow cutting two rings shall be scored as being in the ring of the greater value.

21. Arrows passing through the face, but still in the butt may be pushed back and scored as a hit in the circle through which it went.

22. Bounces or arrows passing through the target may not be scored.

23. Ties may be shot off on first three targets.

Archery Golf

This game is a variety of flight shooting except on the green, when a cardboard disc must be hit to finish the hole. When playing against golfers, archers usually win as they seem to have an advantage over their opponents. However, as a competitive game for archers only it can be exciting.

G.N.A.S. Rules (Provisional)

1. Only one bow shall be used throughout a round. In case of breakage it may be replaced.
2. Any arrows may be used.
3. The archer may " hole out " by hitting a white cardboard disc, 4 ins. in diameter, placed flat on the ground at least 1 yard within the edge of the green level with the hole.
4. An arrow landing off the fairway or in a bunker shall incur one extra stroke.
5. The archer must stand immediately behind where his arrow lands to shoot the next arrow.
6. A lost arrow incurs the normal penalty (as in golf) for stroke play but loses the hole in match play.
7. The winner of the previous " hole " takes the first shot for the next hole.
8. The current Golf Rules and local Course Regulations shall apply in all cases not covered by the foregoing rules.

Popinjay

The word popinjay means a parrot and the original form of this kind of shooting consisted of shooting at the figure of a parrot at the top of a pole. Today the popinjay is more often plural, the target aimed at being bunches of feathers to represent a Cock, Hens, Chickens and sometimes Ducks as well. The archer stands under the pole and aims straight upwards, drawing the arrow to his cheek. As the arrow when its force is spent falls to earth again, endangering the archers and spectators, wooden arrows are used with flat heads. In Belgium, where this sport is very popular, the popinjay courts are covered with wire netting to catch the falling arrows. It is a difficult but thrilling form of archery.

G.N.A.S. Rules (Provisional)

1. (a) There shall be one Cock, a wooden cylinder 5 ins. × 2 ins., four Hens, 4 ins. × 1 in., and not less than 24 Chicks, 2 ins. × 1 in., all with feathers attached.

    (b) The distance between Hens shall be not less than 8 ins., and between Chicks not less than 4 ins.

    (c) The vertical height between rows shall be not less than 1 yard, and a plan showing the dimensions shall be available to the competitors.

2. (*a*) The height of the mast shall be 85 ft.

   (*b*) The diameter of the base ring shall be 5 yards.

3. Only arrows with heads of from $\frac{3}{4}$ in. to 1 in. diameter shall be used.

4. (*a*) Archers shall draw for order of shooting. Only one archer shall shoot at a time.

   (*b*) One foot must be within the base ring when shooting.

5. (*a*) Birds must be dislodged from the perch to score.

   (*b*) The Cock shall score 5 points, the Hens 3 each and the Chicks 1 each.

   (*c*) The birds shall be reset after the Cock has been dislodged.

Bow Hunting

This sport enjoys great popularity in the United States of America where game of all kinds is still abundant. In the British Isles, however, the archer is limited to ground game, hares and rabbits, and deer at organised hunting camps. To be on the right side of the Law it is necessary to get the permission of the farmer over whose ground you propose to shoot and this must be in writing. You should also have with you a Game Licence. This can be obtained from any Post Office. It costs £3 for one year from August 1st to July 31st. You do not need a licence for your bow.

Archery Darts

Archers can play a game of darts in competition with genuine dart players. Their board can be fastened to a 4-ft. boss and it is usual to make this of cardboard 30 ins. in diameter. The archers shoot from a position three times the distance from the real dart board. Scoring is the same as in the ordinary darts game and an arrow hitting the line does not score as it is considered that a dart on hitting the wire would fall to the ground.

Indoor Shooting

Target archery can be practised under cover in winter. Archers shoot at not less than 20 yards and a free hanging back stop behind the target is necessary to catch arrows missing the target. A 60 cm., 10-zone target face is fixed to a full-sized 4-ft. straw boss. The scoring is the same as when shooting at the 80-cm. target face at the shortest distance in the F.I.T.A. Round and the G.N.A.S. Shooting Rules apply.

Shooting at close range is hard on the life of a target boss. Move the small target face to different places on the boss and if possible, shoot with a lighter bow. Teams can be entered for the Indoor League, details of which can be found in the October/November issues of the archer's magazine, *The British Archer*. Five dozen arrows at 20 yards are shot. An Indoor Archery Championship is held every year—6 dozen arrows being shot at 30 metres at an 80 cm. Target Face, to make a round.

Indoor archery can be good practice when weather conditions make it impossible to shoot out of doors. It helps to keep the muscles of hands and arms in trim. Any archer who has not shot for several months will notice how much stronger his bow feels compared with the feel of it when he was using it regularly.

CHAPTER NINE

Making Equipment

MANY ARCHERS GET an intense satisfaction out of making a bow, not only because they like using their hands and skill in this way but because it can save money. Every part necessary to make a modern composite bow can be bought in a complete bow kit and when put together properly, the finished product looks and shoots very well indeed. Detailed instructions are given with the kit.

But bow making requires a workshop, bench and tools so that not everyone can satisfy the creative urge in this direction. Fletching and cresting arrows is much simpler, the only tool needed being a fletching jig. You can even buy a complete " do it yourself " arrow kit. Plain arrow shafts can be bought at a fraction of the cost of the finished article. These have nocks and piles only. The feathers for fletching can be bought ready trimmed or you can ask your poultryman for turkey feathers at Christmas time. The barred wing feathers make the best flights. The arrow shafts are painted with enamel paint from the nocks to about 6 ins. down the shaft. When this is dry, they can be crested with coloured rings to form your own personal combination of colours. Fletching can be done afterwards or before painting, the flights being held in position on the shaft by the jig while the fletching cement dries. If untrimmed feathers are used, these can be trimmed by bending resistance wire to the desired outline and passing an electric current through it from a car battery. The arrow is rotated so that the red-hot wire burns the feather neatly. Arrows can be fletched straight or spirally, the latter giving the steadiest flight. Of recent years, four and even six flight arrows have been tried out but in the writer's opinion they have little advantage over the more usual three-feather fletched arrows.

Quivers

Go to any tournament and you will see an interesting variety of quivers worn by the men. Lady archers are not so keen on the idea of making their own. All kinds of materials can be used from a simple cardboard tube covered with leather, to six lengths of electric insulating tubes, slotted through wood drilled to take them. Balsa wood glued together and painted green has also been used. The point to remember when making a quiver is that the arrows should be kept separate from each other to prevent the flights touching and the arrows rattling together.

Strings

There are two ways of making bowstrings. The first is difficult for a beginner to master as the finished string, although looking quite a success before it is put on the bow, untwists when the strain is put upon it. The second way is easy, and perfectly satisfactory. Choose Dacron thread for your strings and buy it from a firm which specialises in archery requisites. At the same time buy a spool of serving thread. This is obtainable in colours.

A simple apparatus for making bowstrings consists of pegs on wooden bases round which the thread is wound as an endless skein. Take a piece of wood 8 ins. long by $1\frac{1}{2}$ ins. wide and 1 in. thick. Bore holes at either end and insert two 6-in. lengths of $\frac{1}{2}$-in. dowelling for the pegs. Fasten this to another piece of wood 12 ins. by $1\frac{1}{2}$ ins. in the centre with a wing nut. Make two assemblies like this, then clamp them to a table with all the pegs in line, the distance between adjusted so that a string which fits your bow can be stretched taut between the two outer pegs. Remove the string and move the outer pegs $\frac{1}{2}$ in. further apart. Now unscrew the wing nuts and turn the pegs at right angles. Fasten the end of the Dacron thread to one peg and wind the thread round all four pegs the requisite number of times. For a 36-pound bow you will need 9 complete turns, thus making a string of 16 threads thick. A string for a lady's bow of 26 to 30 pounds weight

can be 14 threads thick. Remember that the string
has to be served in the centre and if you make it too
thick, it will not take the nock of your arrow. A
light string gives a better cast than a heavy one but

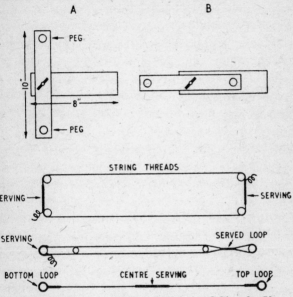

String Making. A. First Position of Simple Jig.
B. Second Position after Winding Thread.

it is not so consistent as it is more sensitive to a bad
loose. There is of course a lower limit to the number of
threads in a string, depending on the breaking
strain of the thread.

When you have completed all the turns, undo the
thread round the peg, cut the main thread and tie

the two ends together with a reef knot. Work this join round so that it comes midway between the two pegs. Now cut off about a yard of serving thread, wax it with white beeswax and wind it into a small skein. Starting $1\frac{1}{4}$ ins. from the knot in the centre between the end pegs, wind the serving thread over its own end and the string for about seven turns, pull the end tight and continue serving, covering the string closely and firmly for $2\frac{1}{2}$ ins. Turn the pegs in line again, slip the served portion of string round the end peg and bring both sides of the string together to form the loop. Bind the main string together for 2 ins. There is no need to reinforce the loops of the string with extra threads to make it the same thickness as the main body of the string. To fasten off the serving thread, leave a gap, then wind the thread six or seven turns backwards from right to left, lay the end of the thread so that it points to the left and continue serving over the string and end until the loop is free. Then pull the end tight and cut it off. A dab of fletching cement or adhesive on the end finishes the job.

Make the other loop in the same way, give the string a few twists anti-clockwise after removing it from the pegs and put it on the bow. Now test the bracing height with a fistmele stick. If this is over the specified number of inches for your bow, scrap the string. It may harm your bow to use it. If it is not more than $\frac{1}{2}$ in. under the correct height, serve the centre portion of the string for about 6 ins. The serving should be about 2 ins. above the nocking point and 4 ins. below it. You can buy a special serving gadget for this job as it is rather a tedious task to do it by hand. Before you take your new string off the bow, wax it well and add a nocking point in coloured thread.

Strings can be made from nylon and linen thread, but in the writer's opinion there is nothing to equal Dacron thread for wear.

Targets

It is possible to make your own target boss if you live in the country and can get a supply of straw, rye straw for preference. The straw must first be made into a rope, 3 ins. thick, and this is best done by feeding it into a 1-ft. long funnel, 6 ins. wide at one end and 3 ins. at the other. As the straw is pulled from the narrow end, bind it very tightly with string. Commencing at the centre of the boss, wind the rope round into a flat spiral, sewing it together firmly with a carpet needle and thread.

Target bosses can also be made very cheaply from corrugated cardboard. This can be bought in rolls 3 ft. wide by 8 ft. long. See that the rolls are firmly rolled, tie them tightly, then cut them into sections 4 ins. wide with a hack-saw. Unroll these strips and fasten them together end to end with paper clips, using a punch. Make a thick

glue with about 2 pounds of slab glue and with a
1-in. brush paint a line of glue down the middle of
the strip. While one person starts rolling up the
strips into a disc, another can be preparing and glue-
ing more strips. Continue adding strips to the disc,
until it is 4 ft. in diameter.

The target face can be made from canvas or
hessian, painted in the correct colours with ordinary
outdoor paint. The rings are best marked out by
fastening a pencil to string secured at the opposite
end at the centre of the boss. Pull the string taut
and swing it round so that the pencil marks the
fabric. The face should be sized before painting.

Target Stand

Three 6-ft. lengths of soft wood, 4 ins. by 1 in.,
are needed. A hole is bored through the top of all

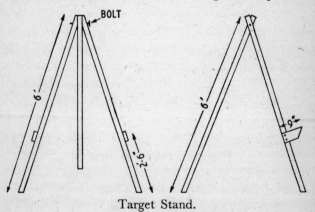

BOLT

Target Stand.

three pieces and they are fastened loosely together with a long iron bolt. The middle leg is the back one. A piece of wood 9 ins. long is nailed on each of the two front legs to support the target. A large nail can be driven point upwards in each of these to prevent the target from slipping off. It saves arrows from damage and the stand lasts longer, if the fronts of the legs are protected by strips of old bicycle tyre. Remember that the centre of the gold should be 4 ft. from the ground when the target is. on the stand.

Target Trolley

A target can be carried on the back with the hands supporting it from underneath. Two people can also carry a target comfortably by using the stand as a stretcher. Simply lay the stand on the ground, place the target on top of it, and lift up, one man at each end. These methods are satisfactory if the targets need to be carried short distances only. A trolley is really necessary for transporting several targets to the end of a big field. Your trolley must be light. Remember straw targets are fairly heavy and three or four targets on a trolley take some pushing. This is especially true over soft grass into which the wheels have a tendency to sink. For this reason a four-wheel porter's trolley with iron wheels is not ideal. The best type of trolley consists of a wooden platform about 5 ft. by 4 ft. with two wheels, one each side in the middle and another small wheel at the handle end. The wheels should have pneumatic tyres and these should be kept pumped up *hard*. The handle, rather like a large pram handle, is simply fixed on with wooden blocks and bolts. With a target trolley of this type it is quite easy even for a lady to put up a target single handed. The stand is erected on the required spot and the trolley is then pushed close up in front of it. The target, which should be face down, is then dragged forward so that the edge rests on the stand's projecting arms. The target can then be turned over and up into position.

Tackle Case

You can really let your ingenuity rip on making a case to hold your quiver, arrows, strings, bracer, tab, etc., and bow if it takes apart. The arrows are best kept slotted through a separate holder made of thin strips of wood and two flat pieces of wood drilled with holes to take the arrows. Keep the case as light as possible as a complete archery kit is fairly heavy to begin with. A take-apart bow can be carried inside the lid and the case divided into compartments for the various items. Paint your box green and put your name on it. It can also be covered with green leather cloth.

Arm Guard or Bracer

Make this from a piece of stiff leather 8 ins. long.

Fasten it to the left arm with straps sewn on at the sides, three for preference, to prevent it from bulging forward in the centre. If the leather is thick enough it can be split to take the ends of the straps. Curve the top of the arm guard and cut the lower end straight. The arm guard should be about 3 ins. wide in the middle, gradually broadening a little at either end. The strap buckles should be on the right side of the arm guard as seen by the wearer when placed on the left forearm.

Shooting Tab

Unless you already have a piece of horse butt, buy this piece of equipment. Tabs are cheap and it is hardly worth while to buy the leather and cut out your own tab. Do not try to make either a shooting glove, finger stalls or a tab from thin leather. It is most unsatisfactory stuff and will only result in sore fingers and a poor loose.

Bow Case

If your bow does not take apart, make a case from a strip of strong cloth, waterproof gaberdine for preference. Sew it down one side and across the bottom and make it long enough so that the top can be turned over the end of the bow and fastened round with a tape.

Fistmele Measure

A 12-in. length of ½-in. dowelling can be marked

at 9, 10 and 11 ins. by rings cut round the stick. It can then be stained and polished.

Tassel

Wind rug wool in the required colours round a thick piece of cardboard, or a book about 8 ins. long, 20 times. Fasten the strands together tightly at one end, then cut through the wool at the other end to free the strands. Bind them round firmly $1\frac{1}{2}$ ins. from the top. Fasten it to your quiver belt with a three-strand plait of the same wool. Some archers add a crocheted net top to neaten the appearance of the tassel.

CHAPTER TEN

Forming a Club

ALTHOUGH YOU CAN get absorbing interest from shooting at a target by yourself, sooner or later you will feel the need for a group of friends to share your pleasure and provide some competition.

If there is no archery club in your neighbourhood, then form your own new one. First find your ground. This should be at least 120 yards long and level. In the country a friendly farmer may let you use a field where the grass is kept short by grazing animals. It is not ideal but it will do and he may allow you to put up a shed in which to keep your stands and targets. In the suburbs you may be able to hire the use of a playing field for one or two evenings; alternatively, you can approach the superintendent of the public parks in your area. He may co-operate and arrange for you to shoot on a football field in the summer months and on a cricket pitch in the autumn and winter providing you do not walk over the cricket table. Help may also be forthcoming from the nearest branch of the Central Council of Physical Recreation.

Having settled your ground problem, put an

advertisement in your local paper and another on the counter of your town's sports shop calling a meeting of all those interested. At this meeting take the chair and form your committee. You can of course run a club single handed and be its chairman, secretary, treasurer, club captain, equipment officer, etc., all rolled into one, but eventually you will find that you are getting more work than archery and your scores will drop. The club may also fail if for any reason you cannot turn up regularly on club nights, you fall ill or you have very little time for all the organising connected with running a successful club. Don't try this one-man idea, run the club on the committee plan, giving each committee member a definite job to do. However, having split up the work in this way it's never wise to sit back and expect everything to run like clockwork, it will not, for remember it is all voluntary work and people are not machines. Just keep a quiet, watchful eye on any signs of negligence and make your suggestions for improvement tactfully at the next committee meeting.

Draw up your Club's Constitution, keeping it as simple as possible and then stick to it. It can only be altered at your annual general meeting. Here is a specimen constitution as a guide.

1. *Name*

The club shall be called The So and so Archers or The So and so Bowmen.

2. *Committee*
   - (*a*) The business of the club shall be conducted by a Committee consisting of a Chairman, Secretary, Treasurer, and three other members, one of whom shall be a lady (that is if you have lady members in the club).
   - (*b*) Four, of whom one must be an officer, shall constitute a quorum.
   - (*c*) The Committee shall be elected to serve one year at the Annual General Meeting.
   - (*d*) The retiring Chairman, or retiring Secretary shall be *ex-officio* on the committee for the following year (this is important and ensures continuity).

3. *Annual General Meeting*
   - (*a*) A General meeting shall be held each year.
   - (*b*) At each General meeting all members may vote.
   - (*c*) Any proposed change to the Constitution shall be decided only at the A.G.M.

4. *Membership*
   - (*a*) New members must be sponsored by at least one existing committee member and approved by the Committee.
   - (*b*) The Committee shall have the power to expel from the Club any member who is guilty of a gross breach of the safety rules.
   - (*c*) Every member shall be supplied with a

copy of the Constitution and the G.N.A.S.
Rules of Shooting.

5. *Subscription*

   (*a*) The annual subscription shall be two
guineas (or the agreed amount) payable
on March 1st (or any date agreed upon).

   (*b*) Members who have not renewed their subscription three months after it is due, shall
be notified by the Treasurer in writing and
if the subscription is not paid by a month
later, shall be said to have resigned from
the Club.

6. *Finance*

   (*a*) At each A.G.M. the Treasurer shall sub-
mit for approval by the meeting a statement of accounts audited by any member
of the Club who is not at the time of the
audit, a member of the Committee.

   (*b*) Club equipment shall be bought by the
Treasurer subject to the approval of the
Committee.

7. *Affiliation*

The club shall be affiliated to the Regional
Society acting as a branch of the G.N.A.S. and
shall abide by the constitution and rules of the
G.N.A.S.

Base your constitution on the above rules, altering
them to suit your own club's particular require-
ments. You may for instance wish to include

juniors and modify the entrance fee for them. Some clubs prefer to admit juniors to shoot, only when accompanied by a parent who is also a member of the club. It is not usually advisable to admit boys and girls under 14 on their own. Remember a bow and arrows constitute a lethal weapon.

A clause concerning visitors might also be included in your constitution. It is usual to charge a small fee for the use of the ground, archery tackle and targets. Prospective new members are charged so much a visit by some clubs up to three visits and if they join the club, this sum is deducted from their subscription. If there is a waiting list this is of course unnecessary.

What is the ideal number of members in an archery club? This depends to some extent on the size of your ground. You can always reckon that about one-third of the total number of members will turn up to practise or to shoot on a Club Target Day. If you have a large ground, you may admit members up to 50. Above that number there is a danger that the feeling of friendliness and belonging to a group will be lost. The individual archer no longer knows the names of everyone in the club. An over large membership throws too much work on to the secretary and treasurer and the newcomer may feel unwanted and unwelcome. The atmosphere in a smaller club of about 30 members is a happy one and the club can be easily run but if the membership drops below this figure, there is a possibility that the club may fade out, the chief reason being that the founder member officers will get a little tired of always running the show and the membership is too small to provide efficient and enthusiastic archers to take over.

Complaints are often heard that archers are not interested in the business side of a club and do not turn up at the Annual General Meeting. This need not be so. Liven up the proceedings by serving coffee and biscuits (or beer !) to all during an interval. Ask members to bring along any medals or trophies they have won during the year. Start a club log book containing photographs, news cuttings and other items of a personal nature and pass it round to all. An archery film might also be shown after the conclusion of the business part of the meeting. These can be hired.

Someone will probably suggest that the Club has a badge and colours. The firm that embroiders the badge for you may also design it for you. Your club colours can also be incorporated in the woollen tassel members wear on the quiver belt, but before choosing the colours of your tassels, write to the Tassel Registrar, care of the G.N.A.S., for approval. This may avoid clashing with other clubs' pet colour combinations. A club gonfalon (banner) gives expression to the creative art of ladies in the club. The club badge is usually reproduced on the

gonfalon and suspended from the cross bar of a pole.
It is taken to outside tournaments when several
members of the club are taking part.

Publicity can play a big part in building up the
membership of a new club. Send a brief account of
its formation to your local paper. If you have a
club championship shoot, send the results as soon as
you get them to the same paper. Make them as
concise as possible, giving the name of the round, the
number of arrows shot at each distance, the names
and scores of the winners and that's all ! Remember
space is precious in the press and your news must be
red hot. The editor and the local information
bureau should know the name and address of the
Club secretary so that they can direct inquiries to
him.

It is a good idea to send a news letter round to
club members several times a year ; once a month
if the secretary has time and a duplicator. This
keeps members together during the winter months.
The news letter can be developed into a club magazine but think twice before starting such a project.
Editors of this type of magazine often find themselves
writing most of it, for contributors, although enthusiastic at first, dry up after a few issues. To produce a club magazine every month or even bi-
monthly entails an immense amount of work, so
much so that the poor editor finds himself left with
no time to shoot ! Don't be too ambitious. Club

magazines can be most interesting and instructive but the majority of archers would rather have a well-run club target day, good usable equipment and a well-mown ground, than sacrifice these for the sake of a magazine.

As the club grows, various shoots can be held during the season and the programme can be printed on a membership card. Most clubs hold a championship meeting with trophies and medals as prizes, a novices' shoot, a clout shoot and novelty shoots (balloon bursting, for instance). If possible stick to the recognised rounds for target shoots. There is no rule against inventing various new rounds and giving them fancy names, but there are already plenty of standard rounds from which to choose and it only leads to confusion and complication with handicaps to think up new ones.

The social aspect of a club can give added pleasure to every member. Hold some kind of party every year, preferably just before Christmas when the spirit of festivity is in the air. Start in a small way with refreshments, games, archery films perhaps or an entertainer. Some day you may find yourself taking part in a full-scale dinner and dance at a local hotel.

Keeping the club together during the winter months can be a problem. It may be partly solved by organising a monthly handicap shoot, weather permitting. You will be agreeably surprised to find how many members will turn out on a raw windy day to shoot for a badge to wear on their caps. Even the ladies will arrive wearing green knitted mittens and with hand warmers in their pockets. Indoor shooting also keeps things going, especially if you enter a team for the Indoor League.

Make use of your County Archery Society. It has been formed to encourage archery in the county. Write to it if you need advice or get into difficulties over your ground. Most County Societies can supply clubs in their area with a coach and usually there is no charge for coaching during the first year of the club's formation.

And when all the new members have learnt to shoot, don't just leave them to it and expect them all to become good archers automatically. A few brilliant ones may attain Master Bowman standard, but the majority do need to be shown the way to increase their scores. Many an archer is lost to a club because he gets discouraged and disappointed when he fails to make progress after his first season. It is easy for the novice to win a prize or two at first owing to his initial large handicap and natural beginner's improvement. He really comes up against competition in his second year and does need some help. If no qualified coaches are available, suggest that he reads books on archery. Some clubs have a small library of these books and a member acting as librarian.

The Club Target Day

This must be organised by the Club Captain or his deputy and one of them must be present to blow the whistle. A definite round starting at a pre-arranged time must be shot according to the G.N.A.S. Rules, that is, archers must shoot in turn, go up to the targets together after shooting to fetch their arrows and the scores should be recorded by the Target Captain.

Only scores made at a Club Target Day or at a meeting organised by the G.N.A.S. or by a body affiliated to the G.N.A.S. and shot under G.N.A.S. Rules can be recorded for estimating an archer's handicap. Scores made on practice nights therefore do not count.

If a club is fortunate enough to be able to shoot every evening as well as at week-ends, it is advisable to set apart one evening or afternoon as a club target day and to keep the rest of the week for practice. It throws too much work and responsibility on to the Club Captain to expect him to be present on every occasion. To obtain an initial handicap number, the archer must shoot 3 scores according to the rules and the handicap is estimated on an average of these. A minimum of two archers must be present.

CHAPTER ELEVEN

Organising a Tournament

THERE IS NO doubt that to win a trophy or a medal at an archery tournament gives the archer great pleasure and a sense of achievement. If you are the lucky chap (or lady), just think, after you have sobered down, of the organisation behind the scenes which made your happiness possible and do not hesitate, if one day you are called upon to run a big shoot, to accept cheerfully.

Tackle the job under these headings.

1. Find your ground, remembering that archers shoot with backs to the sun.
2. Get a working party of 3 or 4 men to erect the stands and targets and take them down again.
3. Arrange for the transport of targets if necessary.
4. Take steps to see that every target and its corresponding shooting mark is numbered.
5. Obtain a distance measurer and a device for squaring up the shooting area.
6. See that Target Captains have a supply of score cards and boards to write on.
7. Recruit helpers to collect score cards and check scores.

8. Invite an experienced archer to be the Field Captain if you are not undertaking this job yourself.

9. See that chairs or forms are available for the archers' use behind the shooting line.

10. If the public have free access to the ground, rope off the shooting area.

The duties of Judge and Field Captain are often combined and may even include the distribution of the prizes, medals and trophies. However, this pleasant task is usually performed by a lady, traditionally known as The Lady Paramount. The prize giving should take place as soon as possible after the shoot. Nothing ruins the successful atmosphere of a tournament more than a long tedious wait after the last end. For this reason it is essential to have a small army of willing volunteers to check scores.

Trophies are awarded to the highest scorers, lady and gentleman. In the event of a tie, the award is given to the archer who has the most hits as well and if hits and scores are identical, to the archer who has the most golds. Medals are usually also given for the first 3 or 4 places and trophies for the highest number of hits or highest number of golds. Medals may also be presented to the archers with the highest scores at the various distances shot in the round. It is not advisable to give medals as handicap score awards, as this practice detracts from the value of

medals in general. Brooches can replace medals
for the handicap winners or other suitable prizes
such as tea-spoons, vacuum flasks, or cigarette
lighters may be given.

The targets should be set up in groups of three,
allowing 8 ft. between the targets in the group and
14 ft. between the groups measuring from centre to
centre of the targets. This makes it easier for the
archer to pick out his own target. Numbering the
targets also helps. If no numbers are available,
each alternate target should be marked with a 3-in.
black spot in the " white " at the top of the target.
The centre of each target should be 4 ft. from the
ground. All targets should be securely fastened to
the stands and the stands themselves pegged down
with ropes to prevent them from being blown down
by the wind. A gust of wind can blow down a
target containing arrows and do pounds worth of
damage in a few seconds.

As it is most disconcerting for an archer to have
to shoot diagonally to hit his target, square your
ground accurately.

Do it this way.

Buy 60 yards of cord and cut it into three equal
lengths. Fasten one end of all three pieces to a
metal ring about 2 ins. in diameter. Tie three
more rings to the other ends of the cords. Peg
down in line, one on each side of the target, two
of the rings on the loose ends of the cord. The

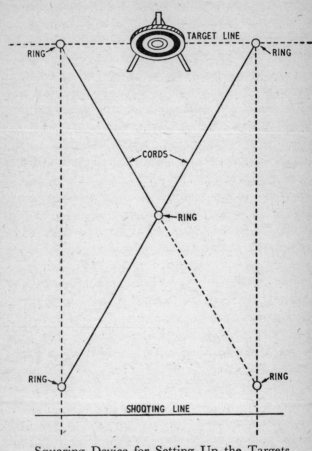

Squaring Device for Setting Up the Targets
and Shooting Line.

Reproduced by kind permission of Cdr. B. McC. Smith, R.N.

distance between is not important but about 20 paces
is suggested. Now peg down the centre ring in
front of the target so that the two cords are taut.
Pick up the remaining cord and, walking away from
the target, pull it taut in line with either of the other
two cords, then put a peg through its ring and
fasten it down. This peg is now on a line running
at right angles from the target line. Measure the
shooting distance along it with a proper measure,
pacing is seldom accurate. If no measure is available, get an archer of about 5 ft. 9 ins. in height to
pace the distances for you. His stride is more
likely to be nearer a yard than a six-footer's stride.

Confusion can be caused on the shooting line by
not placing the target's corresponding mark exactly
opposite the target. If you place No. 1's mark to
the left and No. 2 also to the left and so on all down
the line, archers may easily confuse the marks and
shoot on the wrong target. This is more likely to
happen if the targets are only distinguishable by the
black circles in the white and not grouped in threes.
To be on the safe side, use numbers both on the
targets and on the shooting line, but see that they are
big enough to be clearly seen at 100 yards if that is
one of the distances.

Tapes are often stretched along the ground to
serve as shooting lines but they are not ideal.
Archers trip over them and they get pulled out of
position. It is preferable to mark the various

shooting lines and shooting marks with chalk lines on the ground.

It is not so important to see that the grass is short at the shooting line as at the target end. Here the grass should be closely mown from about 3 yards in front of the targets to about 20 yards behind them. When archers lose arrows in long grass it holds up the shoot as much time is wasted looking for them.

The Field Captain should blow his whistle loudly without any hesitation. A feeble toot is useless and often goes unheard, being drowned by the noise of traffic or trains. He should start the tournament promptly with sighters at the stated time by blowing his whistle. He also blows it to announce the completion of each end so that archers can move up to the targets to score the arrows and again when all archers have returned to the shooting line.

The cry " fast " will ring out when an archer's arrow hangs on the target face, as it might be damaged by other arrows if shooting continued. The Field Captain should stop the shooting on hearing this cry and push the arrow into the target where the pile has struck. Many archers run up to the target and push in their own hanging arrow but strictly speaking this is against the G.N.A.S. Rules, which state that arrows must not be touched by the archer until they are scored. A quick sprint to and from the target is also not calculated to improve the archer's next shot.

The Target Captain should settle disputes about the value of arrows cutting the line between two colours but he may if in doubt appeal to the Field Captain or Judge for a decision. These officials should also check and confirm any 6-gold perfect ends. The measurement of inner golds, that is the distance from the pinhole of any arrow striking the target in a 2-in. diameter central area of the gold, is also the Field Captain's or Judge's job when prizes are given for the Best Gold, or a gold sweep has been organised among the archers themselves.

One final point, if you admit spectators to the ground, keep them well behind the shooting line and do not allow children to walk up to the targets with the archers. Parents who are not archers themselves, often fail to realise that there is danger in allowing a little child in the target area, because archery, unlike rifle shooting, is silent.

CHAPTER TWELVE

The Classification System

ALTHOUGH THIS SYSTEM of classifying archers into various grades of proficiency, with the exception of Master Bowman, is gradually being superseded by the fairer handicap system on the recommendation of the G.N.A.S., many clubs and county archery societies still follow it. It is a simpler system and more easily appreciated by the individual archer as no arithmetic is involved and fewer rounds need be shot before an archer can get an idea of his degree of skill.

The G.N.A.S. qualifications for a Master Bowman Classification is as follows:

To gain the title of Master Bowman, a member must shoot, during the calendar year and under G.N.A.S. Shooting Rules 4 qualifying rounds consisting of 1 to 3 York Rounds (Hereford Rounds for Ladies) of 850 points, and 1 to 3 F.I.T.A. Rounds of 1050 points (Ladies F.I.T.A. 950 points) One round must be shot at a meeting organised by F.I.T.A., G.N.A.S., or a Regional or County Society. The remaining rounds may be shot at any meeting organised by a body affiliated to the G.N.A.S. or at any Associated Club Target Day when a minimum of two archers are shooting together.

Any archer reaching this standard of proficiency and fulfilling all the above conditions is entitled to a Master Bowman Badge. The qualifying scores should be submitted by the archer to the G.N.A.S. Secretary on the appropriate form. The badge may be worn by the archer whether he maintains his class or not, but qualifying scores must be submittted in subsequent years for registration.

No special badges are issued for 1st-, 2nd- or 3rd-class archers, but, unofficially, 1st-class archers colour the lower part of their G.N.A.S. badges red, 2nd-class archers colour it blue and 3rd-class, black.

The qualifying scores for the various classes are given in the accompanying table. The scores must be obtained under the same G.N.A.S. Rules as for the Master Bowman Badge but only three rounds need be shot and it is not necessary to shoot them at an open meeting. Club Target Day scores are eligible. Initial grading or subsequent upgrading comes into effect as soon as the qualifying scores have been made. If in the following year an archer fails to make the necessary scores in his or her class, he or she will lose it on January 1st of the third year.

Remember practice scores do not count towards

classification. It may be tempting to include a particularly good score recorded by yourself on a club practice day towards your own classification but when entering for an outside shoot where archers are given awards in classification groups, you will be at a disadvantage with others whose classifications have been calculated strictly to rule. Every club should have someone, either the Club Captain or his assistant, whose task it is to work out the classification and handicap of each archer in the club. All scores shot at outside tournaments should be handed in to this person. It should not be left to an individual member to work out his or her own handicap number or classification grade as this leads to confusion and misunderstanding, especially if an archer belongs to more than one club.

From the table it will be noticed that to attain 1st class standard, archers must shoot rounds containing 100 yards (men) or 80 yards (ladies). Men can only classify 3rd class if they shoot the short rounds, the longest distance being 60 yards. To be called a 2nd-class archer a man must qualify on rounds containing 80 yards. The ladies are allowed to obtain their 2nd class by shooting at 60 yards.

Juniors (under 18) have their own classification tables which will be found in the G.N.A.S. Rules of Shooting.

To obtain the Junior Master Bowman award,

Bristol 1 and Bristol 11 and Metric 1 and Metric 11 Rounds must be shot. The qualifying scores being as follows,—

Bristol 1	900
Bristol 11	950
Metric 1	950
Metric 11	910

The girls shoot the Bristol 11 and Metric 11 Rounds and the boys the Bristol 1 and Metric 1 Rounds. Four of these rounds must be shot including at least one of each qualifying round and one of these rounds must be shot at a meeting organised by the G.N.A.S., F.I.T.A. Members Association, or Regional or County Society. The other three may be shot on a CLUB TARGET DAY with a minimum of two shooting, supervised by a Senior. The Bristol Round 1 is the same as the Hereford Round and the Bristol 11 Round consists of 6 doz. arrows at 60 yds., 4 doz. at 50 yds. and 2 doz. at 80 yds.

The Metric 1 Round is the same as the Ladies F.I.T.A. and for the Metric 11 Round, 12 doz. arrows are shot on the 10 zone target at 60, 50, 40 and 30 metres, 3 doz at each distance.

County Societies are now organising separate Junior Championships with awards in the various age groups. Appropriate rounds are shot, the shortest distance being 30 yds. or 10 metres, so that even the under twelves can take part.

QUALIFYING SCORES

Ladies

Round	1st Class	2nd Class	3rd Class
American	—	458	390
Windsor	—	549	468
National	—	321	266
Western	—	443	368
Long National	295	219	171
Long Western	420	319	253
F.I.T.A.	741	585	476
Albion	533	421	343
Hereford	650	500	400

Gentlemen

Round	1st Class	2nd Class	3rd Class
American	—	—	490
Windsor	—	—	588
National	—	—	354
Western	—	—	484
Long National	—	316	260
Long Western	—	446	372
Albion	—	556	475
Hereford	—	686	577
F.I.T.A.	850	685	560
New National	291	216	168
New Western	411	309	242
St. George	538	426	349
York	650	500	400

Glossary of Archery Terms

Anchor point. A definite point on the face contacted by the first finger of the drawing hand when aiming.

Arm guard. Part of the equipment, worn to protect the left forearm from the string.

Arrow shelf. Level platform on top of the bow handle which supports and positions the arrow during the draw.

Back (of bow). That part of the bow facing away from the archer as he shoots.

Belly (of bow). That part of the bow facing the archer.

Black. The third circle on the target counting outwards from the Gold. Scores 3.

Blue. The second circle on the target counting outwards from the Gold. Scores 5.

Boss. The circular straw arrow stop to which the target face is attached.

Bounce. An arrow hitting and rebounding from the target. No score under G.N.A.S. Rules.

Bow arm. The arm which holds the bow when shooting.

Bowman. An archer.

Bow stave. Length of wood from which a bow is made.

Bowstring. Cord of linen, hemp or artificial synthetic fibre for the bow.

Bowyer. One who makes bows.

Brace (a bow). To place the string on a bow ready for shooting.

Bracer. See Arm guard.

Bracing height. The distance between the string and the back of the bow measured at the arrow shelf. Also called the fistmele.

Broadhead. An arrow head used for shooting big game.

Butt. Originally a mound of earth on which the target face was fixed. Now usually made of straw bales.

Cast. A measure of the longest distance a bow can shoot an arrow.

Chrysal. The transverse cracks found on the belly of a bow due to compression.

Clout. The light coloured object or flag aimed at during a clout shoot.

Club Target Day. A properly organised club shoot shot strictly according to the G.N.A.S. Rules of Shooting.

Cock feather. The arrow flight which points away from the bow.

Composite bow. A bow made of layers of different materials, nowadays laminated wood, fibre glass and plastics.

Creep (to). To allow the arrow to slip forward when holding.

Double round. Two identical rounds shot consecutively.

Draw (to). To pull back the bowstring.

End. A definite number of arrows shot consecutively before any one is withdrawn from the target. Usually six, sometimes three.

Eye. A loop of the string.

Face. The front of the target marked with the scoring rings and Gold.

Fast. The word shouted by archers when someone is in, or wishes to enter, the shooting area. It means literally " stop shooting ".

Field Captain. Official in charge of a club shoot or tournament.

Fistmele. The bracing height of a bow. Originally

the fist with thumb extended used as a measure of length.

Fletch (to). To put feathers on the arrow.

Flight. Feather on an arrow.

Flight shooting. Long-distance shooting.

Follow the string. A term used when an old bow remains curved when unstrung.

Gold. The centre of the target. Scores 9.

Gold prize. A prize awarded either for a hit nearest the pinhole or for a hit in the inner gold.

Ground quiver. Receptacle for holding arrows on the ground. Often part of the bow stand.

Handle. The part of the bow grasped by the bow hand when shooting.

Hit. Impact of the arrow on the target.

Holding. Maintaining the bow fully drawn before releasing the arrow.

Inner gold. The 2-in. diameter centre of the gold.

Kick. Recoil of the bow after the loose.

Kisser. Small projection on the string to help the archer to anchor on the lips and chin.

Lady Paramount. A lady who presides over a tournament and presents the prizes.

Laminated. Consisting of layers of material fastened together with adhesive.

Limbs. The top and bottom parts of the bow.

Long bow. Old style bow as formerly used in warfare by English soldiers.

Loose. The letting go of the arrow.

Mark. The point the archer wishes to hit.

Nock. The groove at either end of the bow into which the string loop fits. The groove at the feathered end of the arrow which fits on to the string.

Nocking point. The place on the string where the arrow is fitted when shooting.

Over bowed. Shooting in too heavy a bow.

Over draw. To draw the arrow back too far into the bow.

Petticoat. That part of the target outside the face. Scores 0.

Pile. The point of the arrow.

Pinhole. The exact centre of the gold.

Point of aim. The point at which the archer aims. Not necessarily the mark or the target.

Quiver. A receptacle for holding arrows.

Rangefinder. A device for estimating the distance between the archer and the mark.

Recurved bow. A bow with ends curving towards its back when it is unstrung.

Red. The first circle on the target counting outwards from the Gold. Scores 7.

Release. See Loose.

Round. A set number of arrows shot at certain fixed distances.

Roving. Shooting at objects at unknown distances.

Serving. Thread wrapped round the string to prevent wear.

Shaft. The main body of the arrow.

Shoot *in* a bow. Term for shooting with a bow and arrows.

Shooting line. Position from which archers shoot at a target.

Shooting tab. Leather protection for the fingers of the shooting hand.

Sight. Device on the bow used as an aid when aiming.

Sipur. Extension of the arrow shelf on a flight bow.

Snake (to). To slide out of sight into the grass. Applied to lost arrows.

Spine. Measure of an arrow's flexibility.

Stabilisers. Metal rods attached to the back of the bow to increase the mass moment of inertia and to minimise bow movement at the release.

String (to). To brace a bow.

Tackle. An archer's equipment.

Target. Boss and face. The archer's mark.

Target Captain.   Archer in charge of shooting on any one target. See G.N.A.S. Rules.

Tassel.   Bunch of woollen strands worn on the belt and used to wipe mud from the arrows.

Toxophilite.   An archer, especially one who is interested in the historical background of archery.

Trajectory.   The path of the arrow in flight.

Under bowed.   Shooting in too weak a bow.

Under strung.   Having too low a fistmele.

Weight.   The pull in pounds required to draw a bow to the length of the arrow for which it is designed.

White.   Outer ring of the target face. Scores 1.

Worst white.   A prize is often given to the archer whose arrow is nearest to the edge of the target face at the last end of a tournament.